NUTRITION AND HEALTH

WE ARE WHAT WE EAT

UNDERSTANDING DIET AND DISEASE

SO-EIL-026

BY HOLLY BROWN

Portions of this book originally appeared in
Diet and Disease by Bonnie Juettner.

LUCENT
PRESS

Published in 2020 by
Lucent Press, an Imprint of Greenhaven Publishing, LLC
353 3rd Avenue
Suite 255
New York, NY 10010

Designer: Deanna Paternostro
Editor: Jennifer Lombardo

Cataloging-in-Publication Data

Names: Brown, Holly.
Title: We are what we eat: understanding diet and disease / Holly Brown.
Description: New York : Lucent Press, 2020. | Series: Nutrition and health | Includes index.
Identifiers: ISBN 9781534568846 (pbk.) | ISBN 9781534568754 (library bound) | ISBN 9781534568792 (ebook)
Subjects: LCSH: Nutrition–Juvenile literature. | Dietetics–Juvenile literature. | Health–Juvenile literature.
Classification: LCC TX355.B769 2020 | DDC 613.2–dc23

Printed in China

Some of the images in this book illustrate individuals who are models. The depictions do not imply actual situations or events.

CPSIA compliance information: Batch #BW20KL: For further information contact Greenhaven Publishing LLC, New York, New York at 1-844-317-7404.

Please visit our website, www.greenhavenpublishing.com. For a free color catalog of all our high-quality books, call toll free 1-844-317-7404 or fax 1-844-317-7405.

CONTENTS

FOREWORD

People often want to do whatever they can to live healthy lives, but this is frequently easier said than done. For example, experts suggest minimizing stress as it takes a long-term toll on the body and mind. However, in an era where young adults must balance school attendance, extracurricular and social activities, and several hours of homework each night, stress is virtually unavoidable. Socioeconomic factors also come into play, which can prevent someone from making good health choices even when they are aware of what the consequences will be.

Other times, however, the problem is misinformation. The media frequently reports watered-down versions of scientific findings, distorting the message and causing confusion. Sometimes multiple conflicting results are reported, leaving people to wonder whether a simple action such as eating dark chocolate is helpful, harmful, or has no effect on their health at all. In such an environment, many people ignore all health news and decide for themselves what the best course of action is. This has led to dangerous trends such as the recent anti-vaccination movement.

The titles in the Nutrition and Health series aim to give young adults the information they need to take charge of their health. Factual, unbiased text presents all sides of current health issues with the understanding that everyone is different and knows their own body and health needs best. Readers also gain insight into important nutrition topics, such as whether a vegetarian diet is right for them, which foods may improve or exacerbate any existing health issues, and precautions they can take to prevent the spread of foodborne illnesses.

Annotated quotes from medical experts provide accurate and accessible explanations of challenging concepts, as well as different points of view on controversial issues. Additional books and websites are listed, giving readers a starting point from which to delve deeper into specific topics that are of interest to them. Full-color photographs, fact boxes, and enlightening charts are presented alongside the informative text to give young adults a clearer picture of today's most pressing health concerns.

With so much complicated and conflicting information about nutrition and health available on social media and in the news, it can be hard for all people—but especially for young adults—to make smart choices about their health. However, this series presents an accessible approach to health education that makes the work of staying healthy seem much less intimidating.

EATING RIGHT?

"An apple a day keeps the doctor away" is a commonly heard phrase, and although there is no doubt that it is an oversimplification of the science behind the study of nutrition, it is true that eating healthy foods can change someone's health for the better. While it is important for people to pay attention to how many calories they eat, not all calories provide the body with the same things. The foods people eat most often should contain nutrients: healthy fats and carbohydrates, proteins, vitamins, and minerals. Nutrients are the body's power source; furthermore, eating nutrient-packed foods is the best way to prevent lifelong struggles with disease.

The difference between calories and nutrients can be observed when comparing Mountain Dew with hummus. One can, or 1.5 cups, of Mountain Dew is 170 calories, while half a cup of hummus is 218 calories. The Mountain Dew is filled with sugar and refined carbohydrates; the hummus is made up of fat, protein, and healthy carbohydrates—nutrients that provide the body with energy and help it perform all of its vital functions. While the hummus has more calories than the Mountain Dew, it is the hummus that is going to keep someone feeling full and able to go about their day without a sugar crash. In other words, calories are necessary, but not all calories are created equal. Nutrient-rich calories provide the body with sustainable energy. Those that do not, such as the ones in Mountain Dew, are known as "empty calories."

Aside from the day-to-day benefits of maintaining a healthy diet, there are far-reaching consequences to people's food choices that affect not only how long they live (lifespan), but also how well they live (quality of life). Most Americans die of diseases that doctors classify as highly preventable,

It is better for people to get their calories from healthy foods so they also get the nutrients they need.

such as heart disease, certain types of cancer, and type 2 diabetes. Doctors say that preventing these diseases requires eating a healthy diet—one that is rich in fruits and vegetables and contains only small amounts of lean meat, saturated fat, and processed sugars. Despite advances in medical research and countless studies demonstrating the value of nutritious food in promoting good health, the U.S. death rate from preventable diseases, especially heart disease, is increasing.

The standard American diet (SAD) is full of processed sugar and fat and lacking in many nutrients. The Center for Nutrition Policy and Promotion uses the Healthy Eating Index (HEI) to assess diet quality in the United States in addition to how well the average American's diet follows the Dietary Guidelines for Americans. While the American diet has improved since 2009, Americans received an overall healthy eating index score of 59 out of 100 in 2015. Breaking down the categories of the HEI shows that out of a possible 10 points, Americans scored 2.8 for whole grain intake but 6.2 for refined grain intake. Whole grains have far more nutrients than refined grains, so this shows that many Americans are choosing empty calories over nutrient-rich ones.

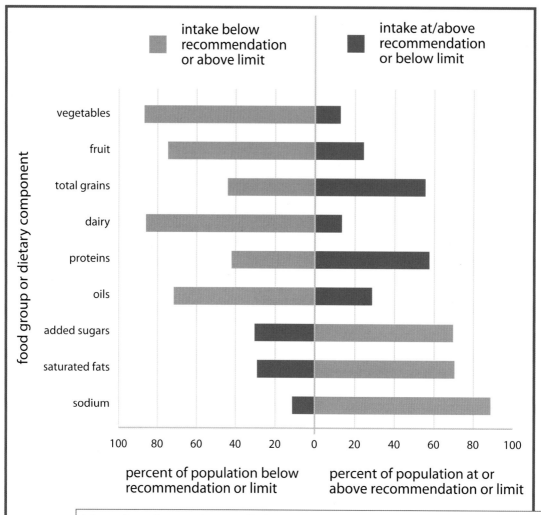

intake below recommendation or above limit

intake at/above recommendation or below limit

food group or dietary component

vegetables
fruit
total grains
dairy
proteins
oils
added sugars
saturated fats
sodium

100 80 60 40 20 0 20 40 60 80 100

percent of population below recommendation or limit

percent of population at or above recommendation or limit

Most Americans eat too little healthy food and too much unhealthy food, as this information from the U.S. Office of Disease Prevention and Health Promotion shows.

Fortunately, the situation is not unfixable. Researchers believe that if people who eat a high-fat, animal-based diet increased their intake of fruits, vegetables, and fiber, obesity rates would drop, preventable diseases would decrease, and people would live longer. Countless studies have shown that a healthy diet and plenty of exercise make people less susceptible to disease and improve their quality of life. In fact, a 2007 study entitled "Turning Back the Clock: Adopting a Healthy Lifestyle in Middle Age" that was published in the *American Journal of Medicine* found that middle-aged

American adults who had been eating a poor diet all their lives were able to experience quick improvements in their health when they began eating a healthy diet. According to the final words of the study itself:

> The potential public health benefit from adopting a healthier life-style is substantial. The current study demonstrated that adopting 4 modest healthy habits considerably lowers the risk of cardiovascular disease and mortality in a relatively short-term 4-year follow up period. The findings emphasize that making the necessary changes to adhere to a healthy lifestyle is extremely worthwhile, and that middle-age is not too late to act.[1]

Preventing disease is easier and less expensive than treating it, and in the case of heart disease, stroke, cancer, and type 2 diabetes, a healthier diet is where the key to prevention lies.

Knowing that an unhealthy diet causes disease is only half the battle. The other half is actively working to change bad eating habits. In fact, according to a 2012 survey of more than 1,000 Americans conducted by the International Food Information Council Foundation, half said they believe that it is harder to eat right than to do their taxes. With the rise and fall of fad diets and the frequent changes in the perceived value of certain nutritional elements, it can seem difficult to determine what "eating right" really means. In reality, it all comes down to nutrients.

Chapter One

FOOD AS MEDICINE: UNDERSTANDING NUTRITION

The foods people eat contain many chemicals, but like calories, not all chemicals are the same. Nutrients are chemicals in food that generally occur naturally and are essential for a person's survival. People eat food to provide their bodies with nutrients, which keep them healthy and energized. After food is ingested and digested, it is broken down into molecules of nutrients that pass through the intestines into the bloodstream. The bloodstream distributes the nutrients throughout the rest of the body in order to do one of the following three things:

1. build, repair, and maintain body tissue
2. regulate bodily functions
3. provide fuel for all bodily actions, from reading a book to running drills at soccer practice

Because food not only allows people to think and move but also to keep their bodies well maintained and functioning properly, it is clear that the food they eat directly affects their health. A poor diet can lead to malnutrition—a condition that can result from an inadequate or imbalanced diet. Malnutrition can cause long-term disease and, if a person is malnourished for long enough, they can die. A healthy diet can prevent diseases, help the body recover from illnesses, and allow people to live an active life both mentally and physically.

Nutrients can be classified into two main categories: macronutrients—things the body needs in large amounts—and micronutrients—things the body needs in small amounts. Water, carbohydrates, fats, and proteins are all macronutrients, while minerals and vitamins are both micronutrients.

Drinking water is an essential part of staying healthy. The more active a person is, the more water they need, so it is important to always bring a water bottle to any physical activity, such as a run, hike, or sports game.

Everyone needs plenty of water in their diet because between 50 and 75 percent of a person's body weight is water. This amount must constantly be maintained; otherwise, a person will experience dehydration, which can lead to symptoms such as headache, rapid heartbeat, sleepiness, and fainting. Prolonged or severe dehydration can result in death.

Active people need more water than people who do not take part in as much physical activity. They also need more calories. Calories are often seen as things to be avoided when dieting, but in reality, calories tell consumers the amount of energy that is present in the food they are eating. Calories are necessary to give the body energy for everything it does—including simply keeping someone alive. Calories are burned constantly, even when sitting still, although the more energetic someone gets, the more calories they burn. This is why athletes need to eat larger amounts of calories than people who do not play sports. Instead of eating the fewest number of calories, it is important for people to make sure they are eating the right kind of calories in the proper amounts to maintain a healthy lifestyle.

A Closer Look

In 2017, *USA Today* reported that Olympic swimmer Michael Phelps ate about 8,000 calories per day while he was competing. In contrast, the average person needs about 2,000 calories per day to be healthy.

Low Carb or Complex Carbs?

Carbohydrates, or carbs, are the body's main source of energy. They are found mostly in plant-based foods such as grains, nuts, seeds, legumes, fruits, and vegetables. There are three main types of carbohydrates: sugars, starches, and fiber. The simplest carbohydrate is sugar, which occurs naturally in many forms in various foods, such as fructose in fruit and vegetables, sucrose in white and brown processed sugar, and lactose in milk and other dairy products. Starch and fiber are both complex carbohydrates, which means they have a more complicated molecular structure made up of many simple carbohydrates linked together. When complex carbs are digested, they are broken down into simple sugars and absorbed into the bloodstream as blood sugar, also known as glucose. From the bloodstream, glucose travels into individual cells; there, it becomes fuel, particularly for the brain and nervous system. Extra glucose is either stored for later use or converted to fat.

Although having carbohydrates in a daily diet is important, not all carbohydrates are created equal. Many carbohydrates are refined, which means they are processed by taking one part of a plant and throwing away the rest in order to give foods a finer texture and prolong shelf life. While refined carbohydrates can still supply energy to the brain, they create two main nutritional problems. First, when a carbohydrate is refined, such as when wheat is processed into white flour to make white bread, the parts of the plant that are stripped away often contain important vitamins, minerals, fiber, and other nutrients that the human body needs. Second, because they are digested quickly, refined carbohydrates cause blood sugar levels to spike suddenly. This causes a surge of insulin levels and an increase in the likelihood that a person will become insulin resistant, which can contribute to the development of type 2 diabetes. Insulin is a chemical produced naturally in the body by an organ called the pancreas. Its job is to regulate blood glucose. Without insulin, someone's blood sugar can either spike or drop to dangerous levels. For people with type 1 diabetes, their illness is an autoimmune disorder, meaning the body attacks itself; its development has nothing to do with how much someone weighs or what they eat. In contrast to the quick onset of type 1 diabetes, type 2

Simple carbohydrates are generally easy to identify because the foods that contain them are white, whereas foods that contain complex carbohydrates tend to be brown.

diabetes develops slowly over time, and weight and diet play key roles in this process.

The complex carbohydrates in whole foods, or foods that are as unprocessed and close to their natural state as possible, tend to release glucose gradually into the bloodstream instead of all at once. A steady supply of glucose means the body will have the right amount of fuel to maintain the normal function of cells. Because glucose molecules are very large and can block the flow of blood through the body's smallest blood vessels, too much glucose entering the bloodstream at once can cause nerve damage. In addition, whole foods frequently include water and bulk, which cause someone to feel fuller for longer with fewer calories. Dieticians recommend that at least half of a person's daily carbohydrates should come from whole foods. In addition to supplying the body with energy, complex carbohydrates also supply the body with another essential nutrient: fiber.

A Closer Look

According to the Centers for Disease Control and Prevention (CDC), fewer than 1 in 10 children and adults eat the recommended daily amount of vegetables.

The Benefits of Fiber

Fiber is the part of the plant that the human body cannot digest, but oddly enough, the very fact that humans cannot digest fiber is what makes it so helpful. A balanced diet requires two kinds of fiber: soluble and insoluble.

Soluble fiber dissolves in water and is found in oats, beans, and fruits. It is absorbed by the body and passes into the blood. Soluble fiber can prevent constipation (difficulty having a bowel movement) because when it combines with feces, this fiber helps hold water in, keeping feces soft so it can pass through the intestines easily. Because soluble fiber binds with cholesterol and carries it out of the body, a lack of this type of fiber can contribute to high cholesterol levels and increase the risk of heart disease. A lack of soluble fiber also contributes to the development of gallstones, which can form from an excess of cholesterol in the gallbladder. Gallstones block the bile ducts in the gallbladder, causing severe pain.

Insoluble fiber, as its name implies, does not dissolve in water. For this reason, it is not absorbed by the body but instead moves through the intestines, pushing feces along and scraping the walls of the intestines clean. By pushing food through the intestines, insoluble fiber helps the body eliminate waste and toxins that would otherwise build up in the intestines as well as elsewhere in the body. A diet that does not have enough insoluble fiber can lead to problems such as constipation, headaches, tiredness, and even skin conditions such as acne and eczema. It can also lead to more serious conditions, such as irritable bowel syndrome (IBS), and has been found to contribute to colon cancer.

The total intake of both kinds of fiber is important. Fiber affects blood chemistry by helping to regulate levels of sugar and fat in the blood, keeping them from getting too high. A diet that is low in total fiber can contribute

A diet high in fiber includes the foods seen here.

to hypoglycemia (low blood sugar) and diabetes. Heart disease, prostate cancer, and breast cancer have also been linked to a diet that contains too little fiber.

Proteins: Building Blocks of the Body

In addition to carbohydrates, the body also needs proteins, which are large, complex molecules made up of amino acids. Humans need 20 different amino acids, and all but 9 of those can be made by the body's cells in sufficient amounts. The ones the body cannot make enough of on its own are called essential amino acids. The best sources of protein are called complete proteins because they contain good amounts of all nine essential amino acids. Cheese, eggs, fish, meat, and milk are all complete proteins. Grains, legumes, nuts, and vegetables are all incomplete proteins because, while they provide some essential amino acids, not all nine are present in these foods. However, combining two or more incomplete proteins can provide the proper amount of essential amino acids in one meal.

Amino acids and proteins are so important because they are the building blocks for bones, muscles, cartilage, skin, and blood. Enzymes are proteins that speed up chemical reactions, allowing all of the body's cells to work properly. Albumin, hemoglobin, and antibodies are three proteins found in the bloodstream. While albumin keeps water in the blood, hemoglobin carries oxygen from the lungs to the body tissue, and antibodies help protect the body from disease. Additionally, many hormones—the chemical substances behind growth, development, and reproduction—are proteins.

It is important to include protein in a balanced diet because protein cannot be stored in the body for later use. Excess protein is converted into carbohydrates and fats. The body also uses protein for energy when there is not enough energy available from carbohydrates and fats. If someone does not get enough protein from their diet, the body uses protein from the liver and muscle tissue, which can lead to permanent damage. Because protein is so important for growth, infants and young children need more protein. When children do not get enough protein, their growth is stunted both mentally and physically, and they may lack energy and have difficulty fighting off diseases. Extreme cases of protein deficiency could lead to edema, a condition that causes fluid to build up inside body tissue, making it swell. Eating little to no food containing protein can result in a disease

Foods high in protein include meat, fish, eggs, nuts, seeds, and legumes.

called kwashiorkor. Kwashiorkor mostly affects children and infants in developing countries, and severe cases can result in liver failure and death.

The Low Fat Myth

Keeping the body healthy requires more than glucose and fiber from carbohydrates and amino acids from protein. It also requires that the diet contain a healthy amount of fat. Fats are found in both plants and animals. Coconuts and coconut oil, avocados, nuts, olives and olive oil, fatty cuts of meat and fish, chicken skin, eggs, cheese, yogurt, and butter are all sources of fat. Fats are made up of triglycerides, which are compounds that include one molecule of a substance called glycerin attached to three molecules of fatty acids.

Depending on the chemical makeup of a fatty acid, it can either be characterized as a saturated fat or an unsaturated fat. Saturated fat is a kind of fat that contains as many hydrogen atoms as its carbon chain can hold. Saturated fats generally become solid at room temperature and most often come from animals and animal byproducts; some examples include meat, lard, and dairy products. Along with the fatty compound cholesterol, which is found in foods such as egg yolks, butter, and red meat, saturated fats can cause a buildup of plaque in the arteries leading to the heart, increasing the risk of heart attacks, strokes, and several kinds of cancer. Therefore, people should carefully monitor their intake of saturated fat.

Unsaturated fat can come in one of two forms: monounsaturated and polyunsaturated. Most unsaturated fats come from plants. A monounsaturated fat has two fewer hydrogen atoms than its carbon chain can hold and can be found in foods such as olives and peanuts. Polyunsaturated fats have at least four fewer hydrogen atoms than their carbon chains can hold and can be found in foods such as corn, soybean oil, and fatty fishes such as salmon and mackerel.

Fats are not all alike, and some fats are more important than others. Two of the most important are the polyunsaturated fats omega-6 and omega-3, known as the essential fatty acids. They are considered essential because they are absolutely necessary for good health and because they are one kind of fat that human bodies do not make on their own. They reduce inflammation (the redness and irritation that occur when tissue is damaged), control blood clotting, and are used by the brain to make connections between nerves.

In terms of nutrition, one of the most important biological qualities of fat is that it does not dissolve in water. Since the majority of the body is made up of water, fat would be useless to humans if it were water-soluble. The body uses fat to build cell membranes (the outside layer, or skin, of each cell). These membranes enable many processes that occur within the cells themselves. Fat also provides more energy per pound than either carbohydrates or proteins, and it can be stored underneath the skin as a reserve of energy, insulation to keep the body warm, and a cushion against injury for many organs. However, these important properties also cause fats to be high in calories and cause the body to store them in case it needs them later. The body is always on guard for an emergency situation in which food is not available, so whatever it does not use immediately, it

The body needs fat to function, but it should come from foods that contain unsaturated fats, such as avocados, fish, and nuts. Foods that contain saturated fats, such as burgers and hot dogs, can cause health problems.

tends to store. This can result in extensive weight gain if the intake of fat is not moderated. However, foods that are low in fat are not automatically good. Including healthy fats in a meal slows down digestion, helping

A Closer Look

According to the CDC, only 4 in 10 children and fewer than 1 in 7 adults eat the recommended amount of fruit.

people feel full sooner and able to go for longer periods of time without getting hungry again. In this way, including unsaturated fat in the diet can be a good strategy for maintaining a healthy intake of calories.

The Importance of Micronutrients

In addition to carbohydrates, protein, and fat, the human body needs other nutrients that the body cannot make for itself—micronutrients such as vitamins and minerals, some of which can only come from a balanced diet of grains, fruit, vegetables, dairy, meat, and beans. Like amino acids, vitamins are molecules—but unlike amino acids, the body needs only small amounts of each vitamin. Vitamins regulate the chemical reactions that turn carbohydrates, proteins, and fats into tissue and energy. Some vitamins can be made in the body, and vitamin D can be absorbed through sunlight, but the majority of vitamins must come from food. Vitamins are broken down into two categories: fat-soluble and water-soluble.

Fat-soluble vitamins such as vitamins A, D, E, and K are stored within the liver and fatty tissues of the body. Vitamin A only occurs naturally in animal foods such as eggs, liver, and milk. Carotenes, however, are substances found in leafy greens and orange vegetables such as carrots and pumpkins that the body can turn into vitamin A. Vitamin A is most important for the growth of bones and teeth, as well as eye and skin health and the development of mucous that prevents infection. Vitamin D prevents bone disease and is often referred to as the "sunshine vitamin"

A Closer Look

According to the website How Stuff Works, Europeans who explored the Arctic in 1596 recorded symptoms of an illness that was later identified as acute hypervitaminosis A after they ate the liver of polar bears. Polar bear liver contains too much vitamin A for the human body to process, so eating it can lead to unpleasant side effects such as tiredness, headache, bone pain, blurred vision, and peeling skin. In severe cases, acute hypervitaminosis A can lead to permanent liver damage or death.

---

because humans absorb vitamin D through sunlight. Vitamin D can also be found in high volume in fish-liver oils. Vitamin E stops polyunsaturated fatty acids from reacting with oxygen, keeping cell membranes healthy, and can be found in both seed oil and vegetable oil. Vitamin K is found in cauliflower and leafy greens, and it helps blood clot, which is what makes someone stop bleeding after they get cut.

Water-soluble vitamins include vitamin C as well as the group called the B vitamins. Water-soluble vitamins dissolve more easily in fluids such as water, blood, and urine. This means they are easily eliminated from the body, so they must be consumed daily. For example, if vitamin C is not consumed through cantaloupe, citrus fruits, raw cabbage, strawberries, or tomatoes on a regular basis, a person can develop scurvy—a disease that includes bleeding gums and a rash. This is because without vitamin C, the body cannot make collagen, which is an important part of connective tissues.

Because water-soluble vitamins are eliminated so easily, it is impossible for someone to take in too much; the body simply gets rid of what it does not use right away. In contrast, the fat-soluble vitamins are stored and

A diet that contains a wide variety of healthy foods is the best way for people to take in the vitamins and minerals they need to keep their body functioning.

can build up over time, causing a condition known as hypervitaminosis or vitamin toxicity. In most cases, it is difficult for someone to develop this condition through food alone, but if someone takes too many vitamin supplements at once, they may end up with vitamin toxicity symptoms.

Atomic Elements

Minerals are elements that are necessary to the makeup of all living things. Well-known major elements include calcium, iron, potassium, and sodium. Calcium comes from milk, milk products, and leafy greens, and it is necessary for the growth of bones and teeth as well as blood clotting and muscle contraction. Iron most often comes from meat—particularly red meat—and is needed in both the formation and destruction of blood cells. It is also required to some extent in all cells, muscles, and tissues to make sure they work properly. Potassium, found in fruit, vegetables, and meat, helps with metabolism—the process of turning food into energy and tissue. Potassium and sodium together maintain the flow of water between cells and body fluids.

People also need trace elements in even smaller amounts than the major elements. Scientists know that all trace elements are necessary for

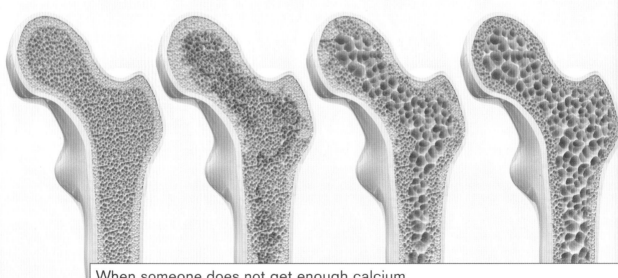

When someone does not get enough calcium, they can develop osteoporosis. This disease, which literally means "porous bone," causes bones to become less dense and therefore more fragile.

human survival, but they only know the specific uses of a few trace elements, such as iodine, manganese, and zinc. A lack of iodine can cause a goiter, or an enlargement of the thyroid gland. Manganese and zinc are necessary for some enzymes; without them, certain bodily reactions would stop completely.

Saving Lives with Fortified Foods

After visiting Honduras in 2010, *New York Times* columnist Nicholas Kristof wrote about the vitamin deficiency disease he observed in a hospital in the nation's capital, Tegucigalpa. In the hospital, Kristof met Rosa Álvarez, an 18-day-old baby who had just had surgery to repair a hole in her spine. This problem as well as other spinal and skull deformities that Kristof observed in infants at the hospital are called neural tube defects. Most neural tube defects are preventable if pregnant mothers eat a diet that is rich in micronutrients, especially vitamin B9, or folic acid.

From before birth to age five, good nutrition matters the most because the body is still developing. In addition to the B vitamins, children have a strong need for iodine, iron, zinc, and vitamin A. For example, a lack of zinc and vitamin A can weaken the immune system and increase the number of deaths from infections and diarrhea.

According to Project Healthy Children, an organization whose origin story begins with a trip to a Honduran hospital much like Kristof's, 200,000,000 children worldwide suffer mental impairment in the first five years of life due to malnutrition. This is a much larger problem in developing countries or areas of developed countries where foods that include important micronutrients are not as readily available or affordable. The easiest way to ensure that people get enough micronutrients in their diet is to add small amounts of micronutrients to common food products such as salt, sugar, and flour. For this reason, the U.S. Food and Drug Administration (FDA) has required flour in the U.S. to be fortified with folic acid since 1998, and most salt that is sold in the United States has iodine added to it. Adding micronutrients to common foods is not only sustainable but also affordable, costing just 30 cents per person reached each year.

Working Together

Vitamins are catalysts, and a catalyst is "a substance that increases the speed of a chemical reaction without being consumed by the reaction."[2] Enzymes are also catalysts in the body, and vitamins are often known as coenzymes because they attach to enzymes and assist in the enzymes' functions. For this reason, all nutrients rely on each other to keep the body healthy. A good example of nutrients working together occurs in the prevention of iron deficiency, also known as anemia.

Hemoglobin, a complex protein in the blood that carries oxygen to the body's various cells and tissues, is made up of iron and a protein called globin. Hemoglobin is hugely important because if the body's cells do not get enough oxygen, a person can become anemic. Anemia is a disease caused by an insufficient number of red blood cells or blood cells that do not carry enough oxygen. It is characterized by feelings of weakness, cold, dizziness, and irritability. Anemia also increases a person's likelihood of dying from heart failure because heart tissue is weakened without oxygen. According to the World Health Organization (WHO), iron deficiency is the only nutrient deficiency that is common not only in developing countries, but also in virtually all industrialized nations.

Although iron can be found in certain foods, simply eating iron-rich foods is not enough to ensure that a person will not become anemic. The iron in the foods must be absorbed in the intestines or it will pass out of the body unused. The intestines do not absorb iron well when it is alone. In order for iron to pass into the body's cells, vitamin C must be present too. Eating red meat by itself is therefore not enough to guard against anemia. It may be necessary to eat potatoes, broccoli, or another good source of vitamin C along with it to make sure the iron is absorbed.

Since all nutrients work together to benefit the body, low levels of just one nutrient can have a dramatic effect on the body as a whole. Over time, a vitamin deficiency can contribute to the gradual breakdown of certain tissues and the development of lifelong diseases. A lack of vitamin A can cause blindness, for example, while a lack of vitamin D can contribute to brittle bones. In addition to preventing the body from developing an imbalance, vitamins and minerals help strengthen the immune system. While some kinds of disorders are caused by nutritional imbalances, others are caused by a pathogen, or germ, when it enters the body. Pathogens can enter the body through the respiratory system, the digestive system, or

Eating small amounts of red meat with a food that is high in vitamin C, such as broccoli, is a good way for someone to get the recommended amount of iron and make sure it is absorbed by the body.

through openings in the skin, such as wounds that may become infected. When the body is healthy and strong thanks to proper nutrients, it can defend itself much more easily against pathogens.

While it is now obvious that vitamins are important for maintaining health, scientific evidence is continually growing and changing both by presenting new studies and debunking old myths. For example, many people have been told that they should be taking supplements (additional nutrients in pill form) to ensure that they get the amount of nutrients they need. This has been repeated so frequently that most people accept it as common knowledge, and more than half of all adults in the United

States take a vitamin or mineral supplement. However, most probably do not need to be doing so, according to a 2018 study published in the *Journal of the American Medical Association*. Dr. JoAnn Manson, the study's lead author, explained:

> The key message is that for most of the population, it's best to get these vitamins and minerals from the diet, from foods. That's where they're best absorbed, and they're in the optimal biological ratios. However, some subgroups of the population may benefit, either because of a life stage that they're in—such as pregnancy, infancy, or

Beriberi and the "Discovery" of Vitamins

While vitamin deficiencies have been present since the earliest humans, the "discovery" of vitamins is relatively new compared to human beings' long history with food. In his 1898 book *Tropical Diseases: A Manual of the Diseases of Warm Climates*, Sir Patrick Manson described beriberi, otherwise known as vitamin B1 (thiamine) deficiency. He wrote that the severity of the disease varied; some people had minor symptoms and could still perform everyday activities, while others could not get out of their beds.

This deficiency was not only observable but also curable in the late 19th century. In 1882, Japanese physician Takaki Kanehiro prescribed meat and vegetables to Japanese naval crews who, through eating a diet of white rice and almost nothing else, had developed beriberi. However, it was unclear to doctors and scientists what exactly inside food was causing—or curing—the problem. After Dutch scientist Christiaan Eijkman observed in Indonesia that those who ate rice with the parts known as the hulls and bran removed contracted beriberi, while those who ate the hulls and bran remained healthy, he concluded that some special beriberi-fighting substance occurred in the hulls and bran of rice.

Though a study conducted by Polish biochemist Casimir Funk to extract this special substance failed, he named the hypothetical chemical compound "vitamine," combining "vita" (Latin for "life") with "amine," from amino acids.

older age groups—or because they have a medical condition that could interfere with absorption or metabolism of a vitamin or mineral, or are taking medications that may have that adverse effect.[3]

Therefore, rather than worrying about absorbing the correct levels of each nutrient, people should be thinking more about ensuring they are mainly enjoying a well-balanced diet.

Having nutrients out of balance is a risk for three-quarters of Americans, including children and teenagers, who do not eat the recommended amounts of fruits, vegetables, or whole grains. The diets of most Americans are particularly low in dark green leafy vegetables, orange vegetables, and legumes. While the human body is resilient and does not need each nutrient to be supplied in an exact amount, it does need nutrients to stay within certain acceptable ranges in order to prevent deficiencies and promote healthy growth and bodily maintenance.

A Closer Look

According to Project Healthy Children, 375,000 children go blind each year because they do not receive sufficient amounts of vitamin A.

Keeping track of all the necessary nutrients—vitamins and minerals, fat and fiber, and amino acids and protein—in the diet may seem very complicated. It is not necessary, however, for people to track every nutrient they take in or to figure out whether they are getting enough of each vitamin and mineral. Nutritionists say that if people eat a diet that is mainly plant-based—including a wide variety of fruits, vegetables, and whole grains—and moderate amounts of meat, sugar, and fat, then they will get most of the nutrients they need without even trying. Choosing the right foods is key. According to Medical News Today, "Nutrient-dense foods are those that have a high nutrient content for the number of calories that they contain. By including nutrient-dense foods in their diet, people can increase the amount of nutrition they get per calorie."[4] Some of the most nutrient-dense foods include nuts, sweet potatoes, salmon, kale, and berries.

Chapter Two

EATING YOURSELF SICK

In a 2006 interview conducted as part of a PBS health campaign, Dr. Steven E. Nissen, chairman of the Department of Cardiovascular Medicine at the Cleveland Clinic, stated, "I get a chance every now and then to see somebody in their 80s or 90s who's been really heart-healthy—low cholesterol, vigorous exercise, really good diet ... Their ability to function and the vigor [health] that they have is exceptional."[5] It is likely that these people have been eating a healthy, balanced diet for most of their lives. On the surface, following a healthy diet seems easy; all someone has to do is try to eat certain foods. In reality, though, it is also easy for people to fill their meals with empty and harmful calories if they do not pay attention to what is on their plate.

Four of the biggest killers in America are heart disease, stroke, diabetes, and cancer. Research has suggested that a healthy diet can help prevent these top killers, while an unhealthy diet—one that is too high in fat and calories or too low in fiber and essential nutrients—can begin a lifelong battle with one or more of these problems. Once someone is diagnosed with heart disease, it never goes away. While type 2 diabetes and cancer can go into remission, there are serious consequences that will remain after dealing with one of these diseases, and fighting them involves hard work. For example, research into type 2 diabetes that was published in 2017 found that losing a lot of weight can reverse the disease, but this is generally achieved through an extremely low-calorie diet, so patients will have to be very careful about how much they eat for the rest of their lives. The best way to deal with heart disease, stroke, diabetes, and cancer is to prevent them from happening in the first place. Nissen reminded people that

we're not just talking about how long you live; we're talking about the quality of your life ... I don't think the purpose of modern medicine is

A healthy diet can help someone stay fit and active as they age.

to extend life; it's to improve the quality of life ... Those are victories that are hard to achieve when you're patching up a disease that's had its ravages over a long period of time. That's the kind of outcome we can get if we can prevent the disease in the first place.[6]

While there are a number of ways to prevent these diseases, one of the easiest and most important is to first focus on food.

Maintaining a Healthy Weight

Being overweight or underweight can quickly decrease both life expectancy (how long someone is expected to live) and quality of life. Doctors generally use the body mass index (BMI) to determine whether someone is at a healthy weight. This measurement calculates how much of a person's body is fat by looking at their weight and height. Anyone can consult a BMI chart—they are easily found online—but it is important for people to remember that BMI does not take into account the weight of muscle. This means someone who is very short and also very muscular may have a BMI in the overweight range, even though losing weight would actually make them less healthy. People should always consult a health professional when determining their individual healthy weight zone. Whether patients are trying to gain weight or lose it, it is important to focus on whole, nutritious, healthy foods to avoid developing health problems. For instance, someone who is trying to gain weight could easily do so by eating a lot of junk food, but these empty calories will not give them the nutrients they need to stay healthy.

Typically, being overweight or obese is the result of ingesting more calories than are burned, but weight can also be effected by genetic and environmental factors. Obesity is not only a risk factor for stroke, it is also connected to many other diseases, such as arthritis, diabetes, heart disease, and hypertension (high blood pressure). Obesity and the diseases that frequently go with it can be the result of eating a diet that is high in junk food along with living a sedentary, or inactive, lifestyle. Scientists have discovered that the best way to prevent obesity is to teach children about the importance of a healthy diet because not only are eating habits and attitudes toward food developed at a young age, but also children who are overweight have a much higher risk of staying overweight into adulthood.

On the opposite end of the spectrum, being underweight can also cause serious health problems. While some people have health conditions that make it difficult for them to gain weight, others are underweight because they simply do not eat enough calories. It is common knowledge that junk food can lead to weight gain, but it is less well-known that someone can be underweight or of average weight even if they eat a lot of junk food. Weight is not the only indicator of poor health, but without this visible reminder, people who maintain a healthy weight while eating too much junk food may believe they are healthier than they actually are. In 2015, writer

Weight is not the only indicator of health. Someone who is underweight can be just as unhealthy as someone who is overweight.

Jeff Wilser demonstrated that it is possible to lose weight while eating poorly by challenging himself to eat nothing but junk food for 30 days, as long as he ate fewer than 2,000 calories per day. At the end of his challenge, he had lost 11 pounds (5 kg). Dietitian Kate Gudorf commented that Wilser "is a really good example that a weight-loss diet and a healthy diet is not necessarily the same … you're putting yourself at risk of developing chronic diseases like diabetes, cardiovascular disease and even some cancers."[7] These diseases are generally not visible and can therefore be harder to identify until they are too far along to reverse.

Being underweight can cause issues such as osteoporosis or a weakened immune system, causing people without enough body fat to become sick more often and stay sick longer. Underweight women can experience problems with their menstrual cycle, which can result in fertility problems when trying to become pregnant.

Heart Failure and Cardiovascular Disease

While heart failure sounds deadly—and ultimately is—the National Heart, Lung, and Blood Institute (NHLBI) reports that approximately 5.7 million Americans are currently living with heart failure. Heart failure is a serious long-term condition that occurs when the heart cannot keep up with its workload. In other words, heart failure occurs when the heart is either unable to fill with enough blood or it is unable to pump blood with enough force to reach the rest of the body. Some people with heart failure suffer from both conditions at once.

Scientists know that obesity increases the risk of heart failure dramatically, but they are not yet sure why. They do know that obesity requires the heart to work harder and can cause changes to the structure of the heart, such as increasing its size. Because obesity increases the body's mass, the body has to work harder and the heart must pump blood to a larger area. When the heart cannot keep up with its workload, it does not just stop working; the heart builds itself up, becoming larger and more muscular so it can contract more strongly.

Being underweight can cause heart problems as well because the body may not have enough energy to keep the heart pumping as frequently as it needs to. This is why people who develop the eating disorder anorexia are at risk of dying of heart failure.

Cardiovascular disease refers to disease that affects the heart and blood

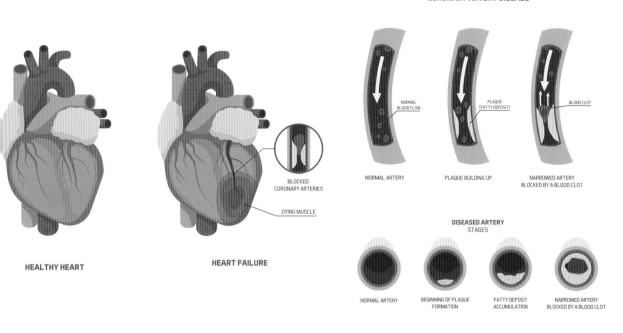

NORMAL
BLOOD FLOW

PLAQUE
(FATTY DEPOSIT)

BLOOD CLOT

NORMAL ARTERY

PLAQUE BUILDING UP

NARROWED ARTERY
BLOCKED BY A BLOOD CLOT

BLOCKED
CORONARY ARTERIES

DYING MUSCLE

DISEASED ARTERY
STAGES

NORMAL ARTERY

BEGINNING OF PLAQUE
FORMATION

FATTY DEPOSIT
ACCUMULATION

NARROWED ARTERY
BLOCKED BY A BLOOD CLOT

HEALTHY HEART

HEART FAILURE

When plaque builds up on artery walls, it makes them so narrow that blood has trouble flowing through them. This can lead to a blockage.

vessels. An unhealthy diet can lead to a buildup of plaque—fat, cholesterol, and other substances—inside the arteries. This buildup of plaque can cause the walls of the arteries to narrow and become thick and irregular, which reduces blood flow and can lead to cardiovascular disease. The most common form of cardiovascular disease is coronary artery disease (CAD), which is the cause of many heart attacks.

Heart disease is the leading cause of death all over the world; in the United States alone, about 610,000 Americans die of cardiovascular disease every year, according to the CDC. Cardiovascular disease includes heart and blood vessel conditions, heart attacks, and strokes.

Two factors that increase the risk of heart failure are CAD and past heart attacks. CAD occurs when the coronary arteries are narrowed or blocked. It is usually caused by atherosclerosis, which is the buildup of fatty deposits and plaque in the arteries. When the arteries are clogged, the heart does not receive the necessary amount of oxygen and nutrients it needs to function. While this can sometimes result in little more than chest pain, it can also lead to a heart attack. Heart attacks are not always deadly, but in some cases they are fatal.

Even with a healthy diet, a person is still at risk for heart disease if they engage in unhealthy behaviors such as smoking or vaping tobacco products.

On average, one American has a heart attack every 38 seconds. Heart attacks occur when the blood flow to all or part of the heart becomes blocked—again due to a buildup of plaque in the arteries. A section of plaque can rupture and cause a blood clot to form inside an artery. This clot can block the flow of blood to a section of heart muscle. If the blood flow is not quickly restored, the section of heart muscle that is deprived of oxygen begins to die.

A Closer Look

According to the American Heart Association (AHA), only about 27 percent of students in grades 9 through 12 meet the organization's recommendation of 60 minutes of physical activity per day.

Because heart disease causes such serious health complications and is so widespread, many cardiologists (doctors who specialize in the heart and blood vessels) consider it to be the biggest medical challenge facing the United States today. Many doctors prescribe treatment programs to patients with heart failure to help them live longer, more active, and more fulfilling lives. While treatment often includes medicine, there are also a number of heart-healthy lifestyle changes that doctors recommend, such as not smoking, reducing or eliminating alcohol consumption, losing excess weight, exercising, and following a healthy diet that includes foods low in calories, fat, and sodium.

Attack on the Brain

Cardiovascular disease can do more than cause heart failure or a heart attack. It can also cause a stroke. A stroke is similar to a heart attack in that it occurs when an artery becomes blocked with fatty deposits and plaque; however, in a stroke, this happens with an artery leading to the brain rather than the heart. A stroke can also happen when a blood vessel in the brain bursts or is clogged by a blood clot. Just as with heart tissue, when brain tissue is starved of oxygen for too long, it begins to die. Strokes are the fifth leading

The Most Dangerous Fat

During the 20th century, food manufacturers who were looking for a fat that would not spoil during transportation and would not break apart when heated repeatedly in restaurants began to use partially hydrogenated fats in their foods. Partially hydrogenated fats are made by forcing hydrogen gas to bubble through vegetable oil. Commercial food manufacturers relied on partially hydrogenated fats for years. They told consumers that products made with partially hydrogenated fats were healthier because they contained vegetable oils, not saturated animal fats such as lard.

Late in the 20th century, however, researchers determined that partially hydrogenated oils are not healthier than saturated fats. In fact, these fats, which today are called trans fats, are even worse for the arteries than saturated fats because they increase levels of bad cholesterol. Trans fats also increase inflammation, which has been connected to cardiovascular disease, diabetes, and stroke. In 2003, the FDA declared that trans fat must be listed on all nutrition labels by the year 2006. In 2015, the FDA released a statement noting that partially hydrogenated fats are not considered to be safe for people to eat. On June 18, 2018, the FDA banned food manufacturers from using trans fat, giving them until January 1, 2020, to obey the new rule.

cause of death in the United States, killing someone once every four minutes. Those who survive a stroke may be left with brain damage, which can cause changes to behavior or body functions. Stroke is a leading cause of long-term adult disability in the United States.

After a stroke, nutrition is instrumental in both the recovery process and the prevention of another stroke. While it is important to maintain a diet low in fat and excess sodium and high in fruits and vegetables, it is also important to promote weight gain or weight maintenance to ensure that the nutrients that speed recovery are being taken in. According to the National Stroke Association, there is a higher risk of poor nutrition after stroke due to problems with swallowing, hand and arm movement, memory, and a general loss of appetite. Some tips the association gives for a healthy diet after a stroke include not skipping breakfast, not putting extra salt on food, eating foods high in fiber (for example, by switching from white rice and bread to whole grain substitutes), keeping fruit and vegetables nearby so it is easy to remember to eat them, keeping a food diary, and tricking the brain into believing it is eating more by using smaller plates and bowls.

Fortunately, the National Stroke Association has stated that up to 80 percent of strokes can be prevented. Lifestyle choices such as eating a

SPOT A STROKE
LEARN THE WARNING SIGNS AND ACT FAST

B E F A S T

 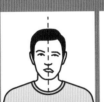  

BALANCE	EYES	FACE	ARMS	SPEECH	TIME
LOSS OF BALANCE, HEADACHE OR DIZZINESS	BLURRED VISION	ONE SIDE OF THE FACE IS DROOPING	ARM OR LEG WEAKNESS	SPEECH DIFFICULTY	TIME TO CALL FOR AMBULANCE IMMEDIATELY

CALL 911 IMMEDIATELY

It is important to know the warning signs of a stroke in order to "BE FAST" and get help immediately.

nutritious diet, getting plenty of exercise, refraining from smoking, and keeping alcohol use moderate can cut a person's risk of stroke in half. Maintaining a healthy weight is especially important in the prevention of stroke because being overweight can contribute to other risk factors for stroke, such as cardiovascular disease, high blood pressure, and diabetes.

A Closer Look

According to the Sugar Science website produced by a team of health scientists from the University of California, San Francisco, each year Americans consume an average of 57 pounds (26 kg) of sugar that has been added to food products.

Type 2 Diabetes

The human body requires sugar in the blood in order to survive. Blood glucose is the body's main source of energy and comes from all of the food people eat. However, if blood glucose levels are too high for too long, it can lead to the development of type 2 diabetes. The body responds to sugar intake by producing a hormone in the pancreas called insulin, which helps move sugar from the blood into the body's cells where it can be used as fuel. Those with type 2 diabetes either do not make enough insulin or do not use it well enough to properly move sugar. This causes too much glucose to remain in the blood and not enough glucose to reach the cells.

Poor dietary choices, such as eating too much junk food, not only cause weight gain but can also make a person much more likely to develop type 2 diabetes. When people eat a diet that is too high in sugar, the body repeatedly releases large amounts of insulin to control all the sugar that is released into the blood. When the body is frequently exposed to an excessive amount of insulin, it can develop insulin resistance—a condition in which the body's cells have become used to the presence of insulin and do not respond to it as well as they should. This insulin resistance causes the body to compensate by producing more insulin. Insulin resistance is a condition that indicates someone is likely to develop type 2 diabetes.

Diabetes is a very serious disease that can cause nerve damage, high blood pressure, and arterial disease. Diabetes, therefore, can be another risk factor for the development of heart disease or stroke. The Harvard School of Public Health pointed out that type 2 diabetes is highly preventable if people avoid drinking alcohol or smoking, maintain a healthy weight, get enough physical activity, and eat a proper diet that includes whole grains and healthy fats. The National Institute of Diabetes and Digestive and Kidney Diseases states that people who are overweight can decrease their chances of developing diabetes by losing 5 to 7 percent of their current weight. Additionally, everyone can lower their risk by making sure to get at least 30 minutes of physical activity a day.

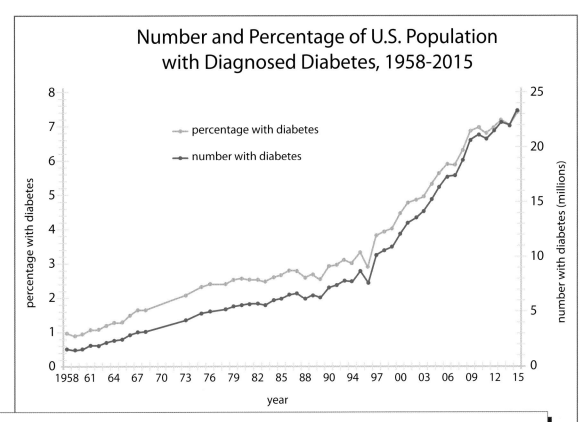

Number and Percentage of U.S. Population with Diagnosed Diabetes, 1958-2015

As this graph from the CDC shows, the number of people with diabetes has grown exponentially in the last 30 years.

Does Obesity Cause Cancer?

Cancer can be linked to the same factors that cause cardiovascular disease and diabetes. However, according to the National Cancer Institute, most of the evidence linking cancer to obesity comes from observational studies with less reliable data because subjects can differ in ways other than body fat. Experts caution that correlation does not equal causation; this means that simply observing that two people who are overweight have cancer is not enough to prove that their cancer was caused by their weight. For example, one might be a lifelong smoker and the other might have been exposed to toxic chemicals through their job. Nevertheless, researchers believe that there is some evidence to suggest that higher amounts of body fat are associated with certain types of cancer, such as endometrial cancer, liver cancer, kidney cancer, pancreatic cancer, gallbladder cancer, breast cancer, and ovarian cancer. Why obesity raises the risk of developing certain cancers is not yet known, but scientists have presented several possible links between body fat and cancer. One theory is that chronic inflammation—indicating overactivity of the immune system—could cause DNA damage that eventually leads to cancer. Some scientists also think that fat cells have the ability to change blood chemistry in ways that lead to the development of cancer. For example, fat cells are thought to produce excess estrogen, a hormone that can lead to an increased risk of breast, ovarian, and endometrial cancer.

Many studies have been done to explore the connection between diet and cancer, but according to the National Cancer Institute, "with few exceptions, studies of human populations have not yet shown definitively that any dietary component causes or protects against cancer."[8] Because of the lack of definitive proof, research is ongoing to see if eating a diet high in fruits and vegetables could potentially lower the risk of cancer. For example, cancer researchers have been exploring the impacts of cruciferous vegetables—including broccoli, brussels sprouts, cabbage, cauliflower, and kale—on cancer prevention. It is believed that cruciferous vegetables have compounds that help protect cells from DNA damage, inactivate carcinogens (cancer-causing substances), have antiviral and antibacterial effects, and help prevent tumors from forming in blood vessels. However, studies have shown mixed results for several reasons. One is that people often have a hard time remembering what they eat and when, so if they do not keep good records of their diet, it is difficult or impossible for researchers to analyze how what they eat relates to their health. Additionally, it is possible that people who eat cruciferous vegetables regularly could also have other healthy

Scientists say that cruciferous vegetables such as the ones shown here may have certain properties that help prevent the growth and spread of cancerous tumors.

behaviors that help prevent disease, making it harder to point to one particular cause. Regardless of the effect cruciferous vegetables have on cancer prevention, eating vegetables is part of a balanced diet and will help maintain bodily health.

When Diseases Pile Up

Any one of the four chronic conditions that kill Americans can be a major health problem all by itself. However, for a person to have more than one of these is not unusual because the same factors—too much fat around the waist, high blood pressure, and high blood sugar—lead to all four health problems. Many studies have been conducted to try to discover the precise connection between obesity, type 2 diabetes, cancer, and

Can Diet Affect Mental Health?

A study published in the February 16, 2019, issue of the *International Journal of Food and Sciences and Nutrition* came to the conclusion that adults who ate more junk food were more likely to "report symptoms of either moderate or severe psychological distress"[1] than adults who were eating a healthier diet. The study reviewed more than 240,000 telephone surveys from the California Health Interview Survey between the years 2005 and 2015.

Similar studies have been conducted in other countries and have shown connections between increased sugar and bipolar disorder or fried foods and depression. The lead author of the 2019 study, Jim E. Banta, stated that, while poor diet does not cause mental illness, it could affect the way the public policy of mental health treatment is approached. For example, improved diet quality among mental health patients, along with behavioral medical treatments, could potentially improve the quality of life for those suffering from mental illness. Banta said, "Perhaps the time has come for us to take a closer look at the role of diet in mental health, because it could be that healthy diet choices contribute to mental health."[2]

1. "Junk Food Is Linked to Both Moderate and Severe Psychological Distress," *ScienceDaily*, February 21, 2019. www.sciencedaily.com/releases/2019/02/190221111701.htm.

2. Quoted in "Junk Food Is Linked."

cardiovascular disease. While there are many factors to consider, one important one is inflammation. Excess weight is one known cause of inflammation, and inflammation causes insulin resistance and possibly cancer-causing DNA damage. Inflammation may also be a response to plaque buildup in the arteries, leading to both heart attack and stroke.

When the same person has more than one of these four health problems, the combined effects of the diseases have an even greater impact on the person's health. This is especially clear from the connection between diabetes and cardiovascular disease. Research shows that nearly all patients with type 2 diabetes develop cardiovascular complications, making this the number one cause of death among people who suffer from type 2 diabetes. Heart disease and type 2 diabetes are so closely intertwined that scientists are not certain whether diabetes increases the risk of heart disease or whether heart disease increases the risk of diabetes. "Whichever is the causative factor," said John McMurray, president of the Heart Failure Association of the European Society of Cardiology, "it's very bad news for those with both conditions."[9]

The good news, though, is that simple dietary changes can prevent most cases of heart disease, type 2 diabetes, stroke, and possibly certain kinds of cancer. Today, doctors, nutritionists, and others who specialize in diet have confirmed that the best diet can be described in a few simple words: Eat more plants, less meat, and less junk food.

Chapter Three

A DIET OF HEALING

Hundreds of people have claimed to find a "miracle cure" diet to help them lose weight the fastest or live the longest. The problem with these fad diets is that they center on elimination, giving followers strict, sometimes contradictory rules to follow. Often, these diets promise unrealistic results based on simplistic claims. Even so, fad diets still capture the interest of many people every year.

While it is always important to be thinking about portion control and considering calories, not all calories are created equal. According to the Harvard T.H. Chan School of Public Health, "emerging research shows that quality is also key in determining what we should eat … Rather than choosing foods based only on caloric value, think instead about choosing high-quality, healthy foods, and minimizing low-quality foods."[10] High-quality foods include unrefined, minimally processed foods, while lower-quality foods include highly processed foods as well as refined grains and sugars in addition to fried foods. While there is no such thing as one single perfect diet for everyone, there are some basic guidelines that everyone should take into consideration.

Is the Mediterranean Diet Too Good to Be True?

While at least 16 countries border the Mediterranean Sea and cuisines vary from country to country, traditional diets in countries such as Greece, Italy, Turkey, Israel, and Egypt have certain features in common: high consumption of fruits, vegetables, and other plant products such as whole grains, potatoes, nuts, and seeds. They generally use olive oil instead of lard in cooking, do not eat much dairy or red meat, and have a low intake of sugars and refined carbohydrates. Harvard Medical School reported in 2018 that, according to one study, following the Mediterranean diet long-term can cut the risk of heart attack and blood vessel disease by up to 25 percent.

Dieticians think that a Mediterranean diet is good for the heart for several reasons. One is that saturated fat levels are kept low: More than half the calories in a Mediterranean diet typically come from unsaturated fats found in foods such as avocados, nuts, and olive oil. Another reason is that breads eaten in the Mediterranean region tend to be made from whole grains, which are higher in fiber, vitamins, and minerals than breads made from refined flour. According to a study published on the *British Medical Journal* website in 2009, however, the most important aspect of the Mediterranean diet for health was the high consumption of fruits and vegetables. "Mountains of evidence shows the more [fruits and vegetables], the better, period," stated Keith-Thomas Ayoob, a nutritionist at the Albert Einstein College of Medicine. "They're loaded with fiber, antioxidants, and they're where you'll find a bucket of vitamins and minerals. The challenge is to eat them every day and preferably at least one at every meal."[11]

A few researchers point out that the strength of the Mediterranean diet may be that it is low in sugar and processed foods. Another factor that could play into the benefits of the Mediterranean diet concerns gut health. The low-sugar Greek yogurt and other fermented foods typical of a Mediterranean diet could help introduce healthy organisms to the digestive tract. Researchers now believe that a healthy intestinal microbiome—an environment that includes many different kinds of microscopic creatures, such as bacteria that are helpful to humans—plays a role in immune function as well as reducing inflammation.

In fact, reducing inflammation is a major reason for the successes seen with the Mediterranean diet as a whole. Dr. Samia Mora, along with fellow researchers from Harvard Medical School, the Harvard T.H. Chan School of Public Health, and Brigham and Women's Hospital, studied 25,000 women as part of the Women's Health Study. One area of the study's focus was diet. Data showed that, compared to women who were not eating a Mediterranean-style diet, women who did eat such a diet experienced a decreased risk of both inflammation and insulin resistance, and even ended up with a lower BMI. Mora stated, "We were not expecting that all these pathways would be affected by the diet."[12]

The Mediterranean diet features many healthy staples such as fish, vegetables, herbs, olive oil, and lentils.

Even more good news about the Mediterranean diet stems from its sustainability and flexibility, meaning it is easy to follow, unlike restrictive fad diets. There are many more food options than most fad diets offer, and people generally do not need to be as strict with counting their calories when they are consuming the healthy foods included in the Mediterranean diet, so they tend to feel less deprived. Most people will see results if they follow the diet 80 to 90 percent of the time for an extended period.

Cholesterol: The Good, the Bad, and the Ugly

Understanding the blood tests doctors prescribe when they are trying to assess a patient's heart health is important for understanding how a diet that is low in saturated fat and high in soluble fiber can help prevent disease. Blood tests provide two important indicators of cardiovascular health: cholesterol levels and triglyceride levels. High levels of fat in the blood are associated with atherosclerosis—the buildup of plaque in the arteries.

Cholesterol levels are complicated, though, because the blood contains both "good" cholesterol and "bad" cholesterol. Low-density lipoprotein (LDL) cholesterol is considered bad cholesterol—the kind that can be deposited in the arteries. LDL cholesterol increases the chances that a person will develop atherosclerosis. High-density lipoprotein (HDL) cholesterol, on the other hand, is often referred to as good cholesterol. HDL cholesterol picks up LDL cholesterol and carries it to the liver, where it is used to create bile acid, which aids in digestion. The body also uses cholesterol to produce vitamin E and some hormones. Low levels of HDL are also known to contribute to heart attacks.

Nutritionists now know that different kinds of fat affect the body's cholesterol levels in different ways. Overall, fat should make up between 20 and 35 percent of a person's diet. To keep the heart healthy, the diet should be higher in healthy, good fats, such as the fats that can be found in foods that come from plants, and lower in unhealthy, bad fats, such as the fat that can be found in meat and dairy products. Saturated fats (bad fats) tend to increase LDL cholesterol and clog the arteries, while the unsaturated fats (good fats) in olive oil and nuts have the opposite effect. Unsaturated fats increase HDL cholesterol and seem to help the blood to flow more freely through veins and arteries. Both LDL cholesterol and triglycerides are types of fat that tend to decrease when a person eats a diet high in fruits and vegetables.

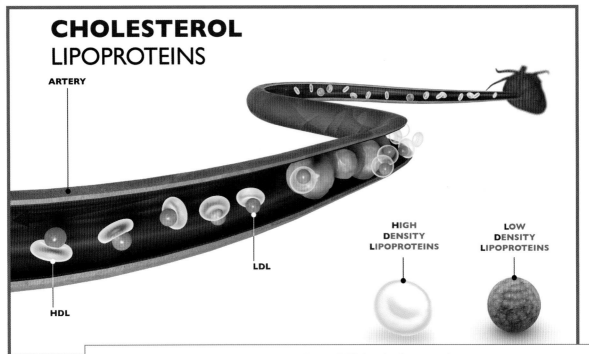

CHOLESTEROL
LIPOPROTEINS

ARTERY

HIGH DENSITY LIPOPROTEINS

LOW DENSITY LIPOPROTEINS

LDL

HDL

Shown here is an illustration of how HDL cholesterol can help remove excess LDL cholesterol from an artery.

To reduce LDL cholesterol levels, a person's diet should also include plenty of soluble fiber. Soluble fiber can attach itself to cholesterol in the intestines and carry it out of the body, thus preventing cholesterol from being absorbed into the bloodstream. Studies show that for every one or two grams of soluble fiber that people ingest, LDL cholesterol drops by another percentage point. According to the AHA, a healthy diet should include foods that are high in soluble fiber, such as oatmeal and oat bran, beans, barley, citrus fruits, strawberries, and apples.

Prediabetes

A diet rich in fruits and vegetables and limited in meat and dairy products does more than reduce cholesterol in the blood—it also helps keep blood sugar levels stable. About 84 million American adults have prediabetes, which describes blood sugar levels that are high enough to put them at severe risk for developing type 2 diabetes. The good news is that prediabetes can be reversed. The Diabetes Prevention Program, a major study of prediabetics in the United States, published findings in 2002 in the *New England Journal of Medicine* showing that a healthy diet combined with exercise reduced each prediabetic's risk of becoming diabetic by 58 percent over a three-year period. In addition, once a person becomes diabetic, a healthy diet and exercise can reduce their risk of heart disease and stroke by up to 50 percent.

The Surprising Benefits of Frozen Food

Frozen foods have had a bad reputation for years, but recently, more Americans have begun turning toward the frozen food section of their supermarket. Frozen foods are convenient and have a long shelf life; furthermore, frozen vegetables can contain as many nutrients as fresh vegetables—sometimes even more. A group of food scientists at the University of California, Davis, led by Diane Barrett, a professor in the Department of Food Science and Technology at the university, were surprised to find that their study measuring nutrients in samples of eight kinds of frozen and fresh fruits and vegetables showed there was no significant difference. Barrett stated, "Overall, the frozen was as good as fresh, and in some cases the frozen fruits and vegetables were better than fresh."[1] For instance, most of the frozen fruits and vegetables had higher levels of vitamin E than the fresh fruits and vegetables. The Frozen Food Foundation funded the study, but Barrett maintains that the foundation had no hand in the design, analytics, or interpretation of the study.

How does frozen produce maintain so many nutrients? The answer is simple: time. Once fruits and vegetables are harvested, they undergo higher rates of respiration, which can result in the breakdown of nutrients. Because freezing facilities are sometimes very close to the farms on which the fruits and vegetables are grown, food can be frozen within hours of being harvested. Therefore, a bag of frozen peas could hold onto more nutrients than fresh peas that traveled by truck for two days and then sat in the fridge for four more days. Since 85 percent of Americans do not eat the recommended minimum amount of fruits and vegetables, frozen foods may be an affordable and convenient option to help them change this.

1. Quoted in Allison Aubrey, "Frozen Food Fan? As Sales Rise, Studies Show Frozen Produce Is as Healthy as Fresh," NPR, May 17, 2018. www.npr.org/sections/thesalt/2018/05/17/611693137/frozen-food-fan-as-sales-rise-studies-show-frozen-produce-is-as-healthy-as-fresh.

The key to reducing the risk of becoming diabetic is keeping blood sugar levels stable and avoiding sudden blood sugar spikes. One reason fruits and vegetables help lower blood sugar is that they are high in fiber. Dietary fiber can help blood sugar levels remain steady rather than go through sudden spikes and dips. Fiber slows down digestion, so sugar from food is

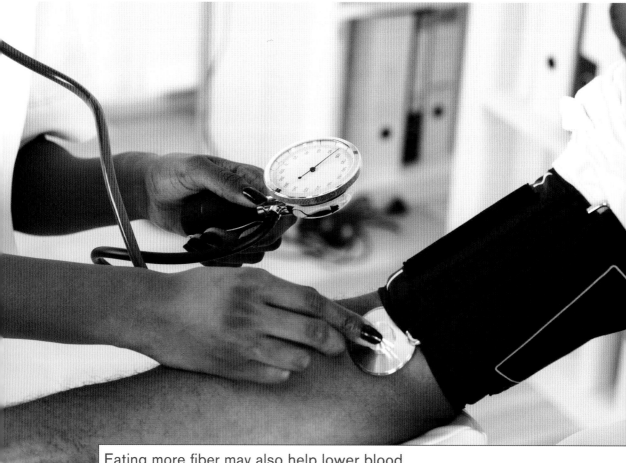

Eating more fiber may also help lower blood pressure, which, in turn, reduces a person's risk of heart disease and other health problems.

released into the bloodstream at a slower, more even pace. Meals that are high in refined carbohydrates, such as white bread and pasta, on the other hand, produce sudden blood sugar spikes because the body absorbs this sugar more quickly.

Another way to reduce blood glucose levels is to reduce the consumption of processed sugar. A 2010 study conducted by the American Diabetes Association found that participants who consumed one or more servings of soda a day were 26 percent more likely to develop type 2 diabetes than participants consuming no soda, or less than one serving a month. Eliminating soda from the diet completely is a good first step for people with prediabetes. Several other studies have linked the high-fructose corn syrup in soda to the development of type 2 diabetes, especially in children and teens. In addition, high-fructose corn syrup is associated with high blood pressure, so eliminating or reducing its consumption may also reduce a person's risk of heart disease.

While fruit can be part of a healthy diet for most people, fruit also contains sugar that can raise blood glucose levels. The one major difference between the sugar in a piece of fruit and the sugar in fruit juice, corn syrup, or table sugar is that the sugar in fruit is digested slowly because it is combined with fiber. Table sugar, corn syrup, and the sugar in fruit juice enter the bloodstream quickly, causing blood sugar levels—and shortly thereafter, blood insulin levels—to spike. Even if the body does not develop insulin resistance as a result of ingesting too much sugar, it will store unused sugar as fat. In the long term, this can cause obesity. In the short term, a sugar spike may be followed by a sugar slump, causing feelings of fatigue, low energy, and depression.

A Closer Look

According to the CDC, more than 100 million Americans suffer from diabetes or prediabetes.

Carcinogens: Killers in Food

Not only do fruits and vegetables help keep blood sugar levels steady, they are often low in carcinogens. A carcinogen is a substance that can lead to cancer. Not everyone who is exposed to a carcinogen develops cancer, but the greater the amount of the exposure, the more likely it is that the person will develop cancer as a result.

Most recently, scientists have found carcinogens in foods they were previously unaware were dangerous. A 2008 study conducted by lead researcher Kristie Sullivan and published in *Nutrition and Cancer*, for example, found that grilled chicken from fast food restaurants generally contains PhIP, a powerful carcinogen that increases the risk of cancers of the prostate, colon, rectum, and breast. In fact, any food that is cooked to the point

Researchers have found that eating burned food can increase a person's risk of developing certain cancers.

of browning or burning, even otherwise healthy foods such as whole-grain toast, contains another carcinogen: polycyclic aromatic hydrocarbons, or PAHs. These are the same carcinogens that are found in soot and in burned wood. PAHs increase the risk of colon cancer for those who ingest them, and they also increase the risk of lung cancer for cooks who breathe them in. However, it is important to remember that there are many risk factors for cancer, so eating burned toast a few times or eating grilled chicken should not cause someone to fear that they have put their own health at great risk.

Scientists have engaged in years of research to figure out which substances are carcinogenic and also to determine which substances help prevent cancer. Research shows that eating a diet low in calories, low in animal fat and meat, and high in fruits, vegetables, and whole grains will reduce a person's risk of the most common cancers. Fresh fruits and vegetables are so helpful in preventing cancer that some researchers consider them to be anticarcinogens.

Phytochemicals: The Fruit and Veggie Superpower

Fruits and vegetables help prevent cancer in three ways. First, they are rich in vitamins and minerals, which nourish the body and make it better prepared to defend itself against disease. Second, they are high in fiber, which helps carry toxins out of the body. The third and most important reason that fruits and vegetables can help prevent cancer is that they are rich in phytochemicals.

Phytochemicals are substances that can affect living tissue in the body. Thousands of phytochemicals have been found in fruits and vegetables. These chemicals are what give plants their unique flavor, color, texture, and odor, and they can influence the chemical processes in the body for the better. For example, beta-carotene, which is what gives carrots their orange color, is a carotenoid. Carotenoids may prevent cancer cell growth and work as antioxidants to improve the immune system. According to the American Institute for Cancer Research, phytochemicals have the potential to:

- *Stimulate the immune system*
- *Block substances we eat, drink, and breathe from becoming carcinogens*

- *Reduce the kind of inflammation that makes cancer growth more likely*
- *Prevent DNA damage and help with DNA repair*
- *Reduce the kind of oxidative damage to cells that can spark cancer*
- *Slow the growth rate of cancer cells*
- *Trigger damaged cells to [die] before they can reproduce*
- *Help to regulate hormones*[13]

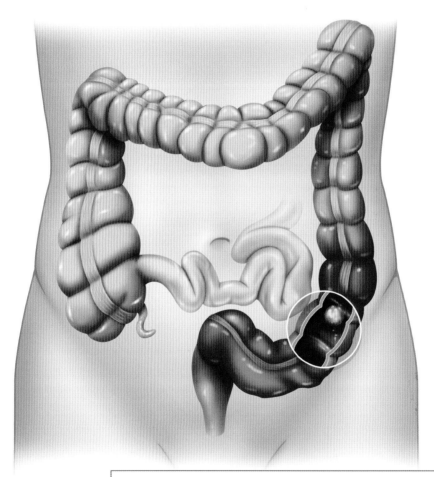

Shown here is an image of colon cancer. This type of cancer can be caused by an unhealthy diet.

The most common cancer that is caused by a poor diet is colorectal cancer—cancer of the colon or rectum, the last section of the large intestine that waste passes through before it exits the body. One of the primary causes of colorectal cancer is eating too much red meat and not enough fruits and vegetables. Obesity, drinking an excessive amount of alcohol, and lack of exercise are also thought to be triggers for the development of colorectal cancer. The same factors can also cause prostate cancer in men (women do not have a prostate, which is a gland near a man's bladder). Many other cancers can also be prevented with a healthy diet. According to the American Cancer Society, about one-third of the cancers that resulted in deaths in 2009 could be attributed to obesity, lack of exercise, and malnutrition.

The Dangers of Inflammation

Some experts believe the connection between food, obesity, cardiovascular disease, cancer, and type 2 diabetes could all boil down to chronic inflammation. For example, losing weight causes an overweight or obese person's chances of having a heart attack to drop dramatically because it helps lower chemicals in the body that cause inflammation. "The biological effects of obesity on the heart are quite profound," remarked João Lima of Johns Hopkins University, commenting on a 2008 study conducted by heart specialists at the university and published in the *Journal of the American College of Cardiology*. "Even if obese people feel otherwise healthy, there are measurable and early chemical signs of damage to their heart."[14] The chemicals Lima referred to—interleukin-6, C-reactive protein, and fibrinogen—are produced naturally by the body in response to disease. They cause inflammation, which is characterized by redness, localized warmth or fever, and swelling. Normally, inflammation is part of the body's healing process. This is why when someone gets a scratch on their skin, the area around the scratch turns red and sometimes feels warm as the skin heals. However, problems arise when inflammation occurs repeatedly in the same area, such as the heart, because it can damage cells and cause scar tissue to build up over time.

Researchers are not sure why inflammatory chemicals tend to build up in the blood of people who are obese. Some scientists think that atherosclerosis may be connected to a chronic, or long-term, minor infection of the blood vessels. Another theory is that overeating foods that are low in nutritional content triggers an immune response in the body, which, in turn, leads to increased inflammation. Even though scientists are not certain why overweight and obese people have more inflammation, they are certain that eating more fruits and vegetables can help not only with maintaining a healthy weight but also with lowering inflammation. Many of the phytochemicals found in fruits and vegetables are also chemicals that reduce inflammation in the body. "People who are obese need more fruits, vegetables, legumes, and wholesome unrefined grains," said Heather Vincent, a professor at the University of Florida's Orthopedics and Sports Medicine Institute. "In comparison to a normal-weight person, an obese person is always going to be [struggling to get healthy] because there are so many adverse metabolic processes going on."[15]

Can Broccoli Help with Breathing?

Dieticians have been encouraging people to eat broccoli for years since it is a good source of many vitamins and minerals and is rich in fiber. In 2009, a University of California, Los Angeles, study showed that broccoli provides additional health benefits. Broccoli and other cruciferous vegetables such as cabbage, kale, and cauliflower contain a substance that protects human airways from inflammation due to asthma, allergies, chronic lung diseases, and bacterial or viral infections such as the ones that cause colds, flu, and pneumonia.

In the study, researchers worked with a group of 65 volunteers. One set of volunteers was given broccoli sprouts to eat every day, while the other set ate alfalfa sprouts daily. The volunteers who ate broccoli sprouts were two to three times less likely to develop inflamed airways than the volunteers who had only alfalfa sprouts. Marc Reidl, the primary author of the study, said, "This strategy ... could lead to potential treatments for a variety of respiratory conditions."[1] However, the study does not show that broccoli always prevents inflammation, only that it may make it less likely to happen. For this reason, it is not possible to recommend that people eat a specific amount to see results. Instead, experts simply recommend that people include broccoli in their diet, especially if they have breathing problems.

1. Quoted in "Broccoli May Help Protect Against Respiratory Conditions Like Asthma," *Science-Daily*, March 4, 2009. www.sciencedaily.com/releases/2009/03/090302133218.htm.

Anti-inflammatory chemicals, though, are good for everyone, not just people who are overweight or obese. "Inflammation is now considered to be a central part of all chronic diseases, including aging," explained Paul Talalay of the Johns Hopkins Medical School. "The same pathological processes are involved in aging as in skin cancer and neurodegenerative diseases."[16] The anti-inflammatory chemicals in fruits and vegetables—some of which are also known as antioxidants—have also been found to reduce not only the chronic bodily inflammation that leads to cardiovascular disease, type 2 diabetes, and cancer, but also the inflammation associated with acne, arthritis, respiratory diseases, and even age-related wrinkling.

The Rainbow Connection

Eating a wide variety of fruits and vegetables is a good way to ensure that a person's diet contains the nutrients the body needs. Nutritionists say the best way to consume more fruits and vegetables is to think in terms of color—the more different colors appear on a person's plate, the better for their health. "Lots of variety means the nutrients can act in synergy [combined effort] for a powerful effect,"[17] explained Cleveland Clinic dietician Andrea Dunn. For example, over the course of a day, a person might have red tomatoes, white garlic, blueberries, purple grapes, oranges, and dark green lettuce or zucchini. One way to include a lot of variety is to eat green salads or fruit salads that have a lot of different ingredients. Another option is to add a rainbow of vegetables to items such as pasta and sauce, salsa, stir-fry, or stews and soups.

"One thing people can do," said nutrition professor Penny Kris-Etherton of Penn State University, "is incorporate more fruits and vegetables into foods they normally eat."[18] Kris-Etherton suggested small, easy changes, such as adding a single-serving carton of applesauce and half a banana to a bowl of oatmeal in the morning or putting roasted red peppers and asparagus spears on a turkey sandwich. She also recommended substituting vegetables for some of the meat in recipes—replacing some of the ground beef in spaghetti sauce with chopped red bell peppers, for example. People who dislike the taste of vegetables may benefit from buying pasta made with vegetables, as the taste is nearly identical to that of pasta that does not include these ingredients, although the nutritional benefits will not be as great as eating whole fruits and vegetables.

Making sure a plate is as colorful as possible is an easy way people can ensure they are eating a healthy diet.

Another way to fit more fruits and vegetables into the diet is to use the approach recommended by the Harvard School of Public Health. Harvard's nutritionists tell people to think in terms of a plateful of food: At each meal, half of the plate should be covered with colorful fruits or vegetables.

Eating a diet that contains a wide variety of fruits and vegetables and is low in meat, dairy products, and saturated fat is widely viewed by nutritionists as the best choice for human health. Fruits and vegetables are high in phytochemicals, antioxidants, vitamins, minerals, and fiber. They are also low in calories and fat. By regulating the levels of cholesterol and glucose in the blood, as well as reducing inflammation all over the body, a diet based on fruits and vegetables dramatically reduces a person's risk of obesity, cardiovascular disease, cancer, and diabetes.

Chapter Four
DIET DATA, NUTRITIONAL ADVOCACY, AND HEALTHY LEGISLATION

I t is important to take personal steps toward achieving a balanced diet in order to prevent future health problems. However, what happens when unhealthy habits begin to outweigh healthy habits throughout an entire country? Organizations across the United States are asking themselves this question and working toward educating the public, discouraging unhealthy eating habits, and encouraging transparency when it comes to nutrition. While personal choice always comes down to the individual, both governmental and non-governmental organizations are trying to make it easier for people to make healthier choices to prevent health problems before they even begin.

Sources of Health Information

In the United States, the main agencies that are responsible for collecting and distributing information about diet and disease are the FDA, the CDC, and the National Institutes of Health (NIH). They also serve as the parent organizations to many smaller agencies, such as the National Cancer Institute and the National Center for Health Statistics. In addition, the U.S. Department of Agriculture (USDA) collects extra information regarding nutrition. The USDA has been publishing dietary guidelines in various forms since 1916. Since 2011, the USDA has used MyPlate to represent a balanced diet. The goal of the MyPlate model is to not only give Americans an easy image to follow—a dinner plate divided among fruits, vegetables, grains, protein, and dairy products—but also to encourage consumers to make it personal and, therefore, easy to follow.

Shown here is the USDA's recommendation for a healthy meal.

In addition to the statistics that are collected by government agencies, doctors and nutritionists who want to get a big picture of the trends in diet and disease can turn to nonprofit organizations that also collect statistics. In the United States, the National Academy of Sciences and the Institute of Medicine are two such organizations. Many others focus on particular issues or diseases, such as the American Heart Association, the American Stroke Association, the American Cancer Society, and the American Diabetes Association. Similar organizations exist internationally. Two of the most well-known are part of the United Nations

(UN): the World Health Organization (WHO) and the United Nations Children's Fund (previously the United Nations International Children's Emergency Fund and still known by the acronym UNICEF). These organizations try to provide information and assistance to people who have diseases while also supporting scientific research.

Fighting Metabolic Syndrome

Once government agencies and nonprofit organizations collect statistics that show a worrying health trend—such as an increase in a certain type of disease or a tendency for people to develop a combination of certain diseases—doctors, scientists, and policy makers in the government respond to it. Doctors watch for signs of the new trend in their patients, scientists conduct studies to try to learn more, and policy makers suggest new laws in an attempt to create healthier trends. One example of the way this process works can be seen in the rise of and response to metabolic syndrome.

Metabolic syndrome, which is very common in adults, is a condition in which the same person has multiple risk factors for both cardiovascular disease and type 2 diabetes. Sometimes called syndrome X, metabolic syndrome is defined as having at least three of the following risk factors: too much fat around

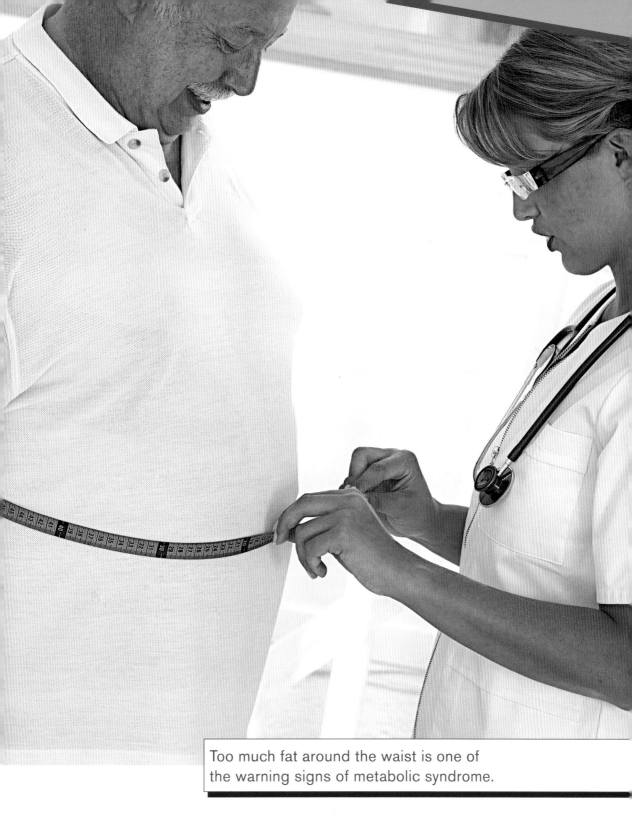

Too much fat around the waist is one of the warning signs of metabolic syndrome.

the waist, high blood pressure, high blood sugar, high levels of fat in the blood, and abnormal cholesterol levels. People with metabolic syndrome are at very high risk for developing cardiovascular disease, stroke, or type 2 diabetes.

Around the turn of the 21st century, doctors began to notice a startling new trend: an increase in the numbers of children and teens developing cardiovascular disease. Doctors previously assumed that heart disease was a health risk only for older and middle-aged Americans, not kids. According to a 2008 AHA study, many obese children and teens have arteries that look similar to those of the average 45-year-old. Some estimates state that up to 1 in 10 teens suffer from metabolic syndrome. In a study of 375 second and third graders, 5 percent already had metabolic syndrome and 45 percent had at least one risk factor for metabolic syndrome. University of Miami researcher Sarah Messiah warned,

> If a kid is age 8 with metabolic syndrome, it will take 10 years or less for that child to become a type 2 diabetic or develop heart disease … So as these kids enter adulthood, they could be faced with an entire life of chronic disease … It is sad because these children are so young and I don't know if they have ever really known what feeling good feels like.[19]

The development of metabolic syndrome in children became a call to arms—at first for doctors and researchers, and later for parents, educators, and government policy makers. Writing in the June 2009 edition of the *American Journal of Medicine*, Joseph Alpert argued that if Americans did not start to make healthier lifestyle choices, chronic disease rates would only increase. He called for government, school, and corporate action, writing, "The time is now long overdue to start aggressive preventive cardiovascular disease programs in our schools, our homes, and our worksites."[20] Taking this type of advice to heart, former First Lady Michelle Obama created the Let's Move! campaign for schools, which aimed to help students eat better and exercise more in an effort to fight childhood obesity. The program lasted until 2017, when Donald Trump took office. However, students can still take charge of their own health by starting clubs that encourage healthy habits, joining sports teams and doing other kinds of physical activity, and looking up healthy recipes to make with their friends.

Prevention, Not Reversal

The NIH is a federal government agency under the U.S. Department of Health and Human Services (HHS) that conducts and supports medical research and makes that research available to doctors, scientists, researchers, and the general public. In 2006, the NIH decided to take measurable action to help prevent metabolic syndrome by calling together a group of doctors—including pediatricians, cardiologists, endocrinologists, and other specialists—to brainstorm ways to reduce the number of childhood cases of metabolic syndrome.

One of the first things NIH specialists decided to do was to spread the word. In 2007, the International Diabetes Federation (IDF) introduced a new definition of metabolic syndrome aimed at catching children who are at risk for type 2 diabetes, cardiovascular disease, and stroke as early as possible. The new definition allowed pediatricians to diagnose children using abdominal circumference, blood pressure, and blood test results such as elevated triglycerides, low HDL cholesterol, and blood glucose levels.

At the same time, the IDF also called for governments around the world to do more to prevent metabolic syndrome. Professor George Alberti, a past president of IDF and coauthor of the new definition, explained,

> Early detection followed by treatment—particularly lifestyle intervention—is vital to halt the progression of the metabolic syndrome and safeguard the future health of children and adolescents … We call on governments to create environments that allow for lifestyle changes. This will require a coordinated approach across all sectors including health, education, sports and agriculture, but it is the only way we can curb the burden of type 2 diabetes and cardiovascular disease.[21]

Scientists and researchers also committed to studying metabolic syndrome further. Knowledge of metabolic syndrome is still relatively new—as are pediatric variations of cardiovascular disease, atherosclerosis, and type 2 diabetes—so researchers need to know more about how these conditions develop in children and teens. Better information, they felt, could be used later not only by doctors advising patients, but also by legislators and government regulatory agencies trying to set policies related to school lunches and health insurance.

Obesity in children is a trend that has been causing experts concern for several years.

Knowing that preventing a disease is easier than reversing it, researchers are still studying populations of obese children and teens, trying to determine what factors, such as weight or diet, might cause one child to develop cardiovascular disease or diabetes while another, equally obese child does not develop those diseases. According to a study from the American Academy of Pediatrics published in the August 2017 issue of the journal *Pediatrics*, it is most important to focus on the individual risk factors. The study states, "Regardless of the definition used, there is no uniform way to treat MetS [metabolic syndrome] when it is diagnosed [in adolescents] other than weight management. Instead, each risk factor must be treated individually, which leaves pediatricians wondering whether they should (and how to) define MetS in their patients."[22] Therefore, successful treatment of metabolic syndrome in children becomes more about preventing obesity, dealing with its associated metabolic abnormalities, and treatment of any additional conditions such as mental health disorders. Being obese can cause issues such as depression and anxiety.

A Closer Look

According to a survey conducted by the CDC, Americans drink the majority (52 percent) of the sugar-sweetened beverages they consume at home. Keeping soda and juices with a lot of added sugar out of the house may help reduce this consumption.

Problems with the Liver

Liver disease used to be mainly caused by drinking too much alcohol. The liver is the organ that is responsible for filtering toxins—such as alcohol—out of the blood. When adults die of liver failure after a lifetime of alcohol abuse, it is because they drank to excess so many times that their livers became unable to keep filtering those toxins out of their blood. However, the liver has another job: It also helps the body digest fat. As more and more Americans become obese, doctors are seeing a rise in nonalcoholic fatty liver disease (NAFLD).

NAFLD is diagnosed when more than 5 percent of the liver's weight is liver fat. This disease is closely linked with insulin resistance. Studies show that 10 to 20 percent of U.S. children between the ages of two and nineteen have NAFLD, although numbers are not exact. It can be hard to diagnose since it does not show many symptoms. Many will develop cirrhosis of the liver—a condition in which the liver is repeatedly damaged and scar tissue replaces much of the liver's healthy tissue—as a result of NAFLD. Eventually, the liver cannot function anymore. Cirrhosis can be fatal for someone who does not get a liver transplant. Children and teens with NAFLD are more than 13 times as likely as children who do not have this disorder to die within 20 years or to find themselves in need of a liver transplant.

Realizing that children were experiencing liver and cardiovascular damage, as well as being at risk for type 2 diabetes and certain kinds of cancer, made children's health advocates more determined to create change. They began to call upon governments to take concrete action to prevent these diseases, such as providing nutrition information for consumers and improving school lunches.

Creating an Informed Population

One action health advocates requested of the government was to make nutrition information more easily available to the public. In 2004, the USDA launched a new website devoted to nutrition. It is designed to pull together nutrition information from several government agencies onto one platform that can be accessed by the public. Former agriculture secretary Ann Veneman explained that members of the public needed access to reliable information about nutrition in order to make informed choices about diet. The new website includes specialized information about nutrition for men, women, and children of various ages and also gives information about dietary supplements, food assistance programs, and nutrients, as well as shopping, cooking, and meal planning.

Another action designed to provide nutrition information to the public was to change the labels that manufacturers are required to put on food packages. Nutrition information has been included on food packages for many years, but Congress periodically passes laws changing the requirements. Food manufacturers are required to list a food's ingredients on the label. In addition, Congress passed a law in 2004 requiring

Nutrition Facts

8 servings per container

Serving size   2/3 Cup (56g)

Amount per serving

Calories   210

	% Daily Value*
Total Fat 1g	1%
Saturated Fat 0g	0%
Trans Fat 0g	
Cholesterol 0mg	0%
Sodium 0mg	0%
Total Carbohydrate 44g	16%
Dietary Fiber 2g	7%
Total Sugars 2g	
Includes 0g Added Sugars	0%
Protein 7g	
Vitamin D 0mcg	0%
Calcium 0mg	0%
Iron 0.6mg	4%
Potassium 100mg	2%

* The % Daily Value (DV) tells you how much a nutrient in a serving of food contributes to a daily diet. 2,000 calories a day is used for general nutrition advice.

Nutrition facts are a requirement on almost all packaged food.

labels to list any major food allergens (milk, eggs, fish, shellfish, tree nuts, wheat, peanuts, or soybeans) that are included in a food. The nutrition facts on a food's label must include total calories per serving and the amount of fat, protein, fiber, and carbohydrates in a food. Packages also list the percentage of the recommended daily allowance of various vitamins and minerals a food contains.

In 2016, the FDA changed label requirements once again to require the inclusion of "added sugars" because research shows that it is difficult to meet nutrient needs within calorie constraints if 10 percent or more of the calories a person takes in come from added sugar. Furthermore, the section "calories from fat" is being removed from nutrition labels because research has shown that the type of fat a person eats is more important than the amount of fat. Daily values for some nutrients, such as sodium, dietary fiber, and vitamin D, are also being updated. All manufacturers will be required to follow these new regulations by January 1, 2021.

Encouraging Healthy Choices for Life

National school lunch legislation has existed since 1946, when Congress first passed the National School Lunch Act. At the time, it was intended par-

Working to bring healthier lunches into schools that feature more fruits, vegetables, and whole grains could encourage children to develop healthier habits at a young age and remain healthy eaters throughout their lives.

tially to help give children proper nutrition and partially to ensure a market for crops produced by American farmers. The lunch program was expanded with the passage of the Child Nutrition Act of 1966, when a milk program and a breakfast program were added. However, many critics today have pointed a finger at school lunches as a major cause of both health problems and a lack of nutritional knowledge in American kids and teens. Part of the reason for this is that it is easier and cheaper to cook for a lot of people when the food is processed, so many schools choose price and convenience over nutrition.

Children consume about half of their daily calories at school; for some low-income students, school lunch may be the only real meal they have access to daily. In 2010, Congress passed the Healthy, Hunger-Free

How Can School Lunches Become Healthier?

Activists such as chef Ann Cooper have been advocating for changes in school lunch programs for many years. Cooper has developed many programs focused on bringing healthy food to school cafeterias, the most prominent of which is the Lunch Box project. The Lunch Box is an online resource designed to help school food service teams make the switch from processed foods to cooking with fresh ingredients and creating meals from scratch. Users have free access to recipes, USDA-compliant menus, financial calculators, strategies for implementing salad bars and breakfast options, marketing tools, and more.

Cooper and others with similar views are hopeful that her idea will catch on. One sign that the Lunch Box was being met with success came in 2009 when Cooper was invited to a conference of the School Nutrition Association. Supporters of Cooper's project include Senator Kirsten Gillibrand of New York, who commented, "If you feed a kid chicken nuggets and canned peas and Doritos and canned fruit as a school lunch or you feed him grilled chicken, steamed broccoli and fresh fruits and a whole grain roll, the difference is night and day."[1]

1. Quoted in Kim Severson, "Stars Aligning on School Lunches," New York Times, August 18, 2009. www.nytimes.com/2009/08/19/dining/19school.html.

Kids Act, which required the USDA to change school lunch standards to more closely align with the dietary guidelines for Americans. The act called for more whole grains, fruits, vegetables, and low-fat milk products, as well as foods with less sodium and fat. However, in 2019, the Trump administration—most notably Agriculture Secretary Sonny Perdue—changed the way the 2010 law is implemented, allowing schools to serve foods with more sodium as well as fewer whole-grain foods.

A Closer Look

In 2017, the National School Lunch Program provided lunch to more than 30.4 million U.S. children and teenagers every school day.

Although Perdue claimed these changes would allow schools to serve foods kids would be more likely to eat, a report by Bloomberg suggested that the new rules were put in place mainly to benefit large agricultural businesses, especially the dairy industry, that make a lot of money selling their foods—which are not always the healthiest options—to schools.

Making Better Choices at Chain Restaurants

On May 7, 2018, the FDA started requiring chain restaurants or food suppliers that meet certain criteria—having 20 or more locations that do business under the same name and offer almost entirely the same menu items at each location—to list nutritional information on their menus and websites. While some may wonder why it is important for restaurants to list the number of calories in each of the meals they offer, the information can actually help a lot in making a more educated meal choice.

At least a third of the calories consumed by Americans come from restaurant food. Making nutritional information highly visible often encourages restaurants to make their signature, high-calorie dishes healthier so people will be more likely to order them. For example, the chicken and broccoli pasta dish at Ruby Tuesday's was reduced from 2,060 calories in 2012 to 1,405 calories in 2018. Calorie counts are also important because menu descriptions can be misleading. The chicken and broccoli pasta, for instance, appears to be a healthy choice because it contains vegetables and white meat chicken. However, before its calories were reduced, that single meal contained more calories

Dishes such as this one may appear healthy because they contain vegetables and protein, but refined grains and sauces with high fat content can give chain restaurant menu items a surprisingly high calorie count.

than it is recommended for some people to eat in an entire day. The sauces a meal contains as well as the way it is cooked make a great deal of difference; for example, baked vegetables are healthier than those that are fried in butter. However, it is often difficult or impossible to tell from a simple menu description whether a meal is cooked in a healthy or unhealthy way.

The Great Taxation Experiment

A February 2019 report from the University of California, Berkeley, stated that in the three years since a penny-per-ounce tax was introduced on sugary drinks such as soda, the consumption of those drinks dropped 52 percent among low-income residents of Berkeley—the residents most affected by diabetes and cardiovascular disease. The results of this study, which was the first to document the long-term impacts of a soda tax, suggest that taxation could be an effective way to decrease soda consumption and encourage healthy eating habits. The majority of the money that comes from the soda tax goes toward supporting nutritional education and gardening initiatives in Berkeley schools and to local organizations working to encourage healthy behavior within the community.

According to Kristine Madsen, the faculty director of the Berkeley Food Institute in UC Berkeley's School of Public Health, "Sugar-sweetened beverages, which are linked to obesity, diabetes, and cardiovascular disease, cost our nation billions of dollars each year, but they are super-cheap. They'd cost much more if the health care costs were actually included in the price of soda."[1] While many believe that it is not the role of the government to police citizens' beverage choices, Madsen encourages people to think about the benefits of a soda tax as a balance to corporate advertising, which encourages people to buy certain foods and drinks. She explained, "We need consistent messaging and interventions that make healthier foods desirable, accessible and affordable."[2]

1. Quoted in "Three Years into Soda Tax, Sugary Drink Consumption Down More than 50 Percent in Berkeley," *ScienceDaily*, February 21, 2019. www.sciencedaily.com/releases/2019/02/190221172056.htm.

2. Quoted in "Three Years into Soda Tax," *ScienceDaily*.

Working to Solve World Hunger

While American consumers debate which sandwich to buy from a fast food restaurant, children and teens in many developing countries are still dying of diseases that are either caused by or made much worse by a lack of calories and protein. The UN contains several agencies that collect information and create policies that are intended to provide more nutritious food and help people around the world battle hunger and malnutrition. One of the leading agencies to fight starvation worldwide is the UN's Food and Agriculture Organization (FAO), which fights starvation by providing tools and seeds for farmers in developing nations and by finding solutions to problems that arise in agriculture, fishing, and forestry. The FAO also fights against poverty by helping farmers and fishers make good marketing decisions.

Since 2017, the FAO has been helping educate and provide resources for tilapia fishers in the Philippines. Filipinos rely on food that comes from the water—especially tilapia—to provide affordable protein. However, "The Philippines is among the most vulnerable countries to extreme weather events and climate-related disasters … Its key tilapia-producing provinces are regularly exposed to inclement weather systems and associated hazards like flooding or prolonged dry periods."[23] The FAO has been working with Filipino fishers and scientists to educate and train both groups on how to combine weather knowledge with fishing practices. For example, automatic weather stations have been installed that provide a web-based platform to send text alerts to tilapia fishers in the event of thunderstorms, heavy rains, and extreme temperatures—all factors that affect the fishermen's safety and productivity.

Chapter Five
FOOD EDUCATION

The global food network tends to promote quantity over quality—advertising how much food someone can acquire at one meal or in one package rather than the nutritional quality of the food—and to showcase ultra-processed foods such as sugary cereals and chips that have not only been stripped of valuable nutrients but also are full of fat, sugar, and salt. When this is the food that is readily available, people end up becoming both overweight and undernourished.

How can society eliminate the dependence on over-sugared, over-processed, unhealthy food? Many believe the answer lies with knowing where the food they consume actually comes from. According to the marketing firm Packaged Facts, the local food industry—roughly defined as food produced in the consumer's geographic region—generated $12 billion in sales in the year 2014 and has only grown since. Packaged Facts predicted that by the end of the year 2019, local foods would generate close to $20 billion. The American Farmland Trust also states that between the years 1994 and 2014, the number of farmers' markets across the United States increased by 371 percent. Furthermore, since the American Farmland Trust's start in 1980, 6.5 million acres of farm and ranch land have been permanently protected from development. Americans have begun to choose local food more often, but how much of an impact does the local food trend have on diet-related disease?

Eating Local: More Than a Fad

While the concept of eating locally has become increasingly trendy in the new millennium, there is more to the local movement than overpriced heirloom tomatoes and craft zucchini noodles. While there is no direct evidence that local foods in particular are better for a person's health, the habits developed by eating locally are where the healthy effects truly lie. When someone eats locally, they consume a lot more fruits, vegetables, and beans, much less meat, and essentially no processed foods. There is also a level of control given to the consumer when buying locally sourced items. Often, buying local foods means meeting the farmer who grew the fruits and vegetables or raised the animals providing customers with meat, eggs, milk, butter, and other goods. By knowing the farmer, the consumer generally also learns about the farming methods used. They gain a better idea of the soil quality, animal feed, humane raising practices, sustainability, and types of pesticides used.

While local food is certainly trendy and healthy, it also packs flavor. Fruits and vegetables begin losing nutrients within 24 hours of being harvested, so if a tomato from California is going to be sold in New York, it needs to be harvested before it is ripe so it does not rot before it reaches the shelf. Therefore, a lot of produce ripens on trucks rather than on the plant, losing both flavor and nutrients in the process. Food produced locally does not have to travel far before being eaten. Therefore, local foods are harvested at their peak ripeness, ensuring maximum flavor as well as maximum nutrients delivered to the consumer.

A Closer Look

Many people believe that eating locally produced honey can improve seasonal allergies. However, studies have shown that there is no scientific proof behind this claim.

Eating locally does come with some setbacks, especially when someone lives in an area that experiences harsh winters. However, people in those areas can still experience benefits by eating locally as often as possible. While local produce is limited to what is in season, and that could mean

Fruits and vegetables such as these are frequently found at farmers' markets.

consumers are not able to buy exactly what they want at all times of the year, it may open people's eyes to different kinds of food they have never tried. The broader their fruit and vegetable horizons, the wider the range of nutrients, antioxidants, and phytochemicals they receive. Someone may even discover a new favorite food or learn how to make their favorite meal with some fruit and veggie substitutions.

The Changing Face of Agriculture

As the local food movement grows in popularity, the face of agriculture is beginning to change. While there are plenty of large corporations running factory farms across the United States, the demand for local food has given rise to a new wave of young farmers who focus mainly on sustainability to ensure both usable farmland for the next generation and healthy produce for today's customers. Although there are not enough farmers entering the industry to make up for the number of farmers leaving the industry—according to the USDA, between 2007 and 2012, 2,384 farmers between the ages of 25 and 34 joined the ranks, while nearly 100,000 farmers between the ages of 45 and 54 exited the industry—many hope this trending influx of young farmers will solidify the presence of small and midsize farms in the looming face of the big farm industry.

These young farmers are focused on providing high-quality food to local consumers through direct sales at farmers' markets and community-supported agriculture programs (CSAs) or by providing ingredients to local restaurants. Most of them do not come from agricultural households; instead, they often hold college degrees in fields such as biology, environmental studies, chemistry, and even economics and community development. Although farming has historically been a male-dominated field, a large number of new young farmers are women. About 301 million acres of land—a third of the total farmland in the United States—is either farmed or co-farmed by women. These young farmers want to make a change in the world. According to Liz Whitehurst, who left a job with a nonprofit in Washington, D.C., to take over Owl's Nest Farm in Upper Marlboro, Maryland, "I wanted to have a positive impact, and that just felt very distant in my other jobs out of college. In farming, on the other hand, you make a difference. Your impact is immediate."[24] While many of these young farmers did not choose their career path until they were 20 or 30, there could be even more benefits in encouraging children to form a connection to the land from a young age.

Some young adults are also working on farms around the world in exchange for a place to stay while they travel and the opportunity to learn about organic farming. World Wide Opportunities on Organic Farms (WWOOF) connects young travelers with farmers around the world who teach them sustainable living and organic farming practices.

Many young people—especially women— have started turning to farming as a career.

Getting Kids in the Garden

Multiple studies conducted since 2000 suggest that children who grow their own food are not only more likely to eat fruits and vegetables, but also are likely to express a preference for fruits and vegetables throughout their lives and have a stronger grasp on nutrition as they age. While encouraging children to garden at home is valuable, it is equally valuable for schools to offer gardening programs.

According to the Harvard Graduate School of Education, most children receive only 3.4 hours of nutrition education per year, yet it takes between 35 and 50 hours of nutrition education per year to enact long-term change in food mentality and developing healthier eating habits. Using a garden for nutritional education can provide an opportunity for hands-on learning. Maintaining a school garden requires nearly constant planning and maintenance, which means it becomes a consistent part of a student's life. When a student works in a garden over the course of an entire year or more, they develop an emotional connection to the land and the food—the kind of relationship that creates real change in a young person's eating habits and preferences. Michelle Obama championed this idea by creating a garden at the White House and inviting local students to help plant and harvest the food—a tradition Melania Trump carried on after she became First Lady. A White House spokesperson also stated that fresh food from the garden is regularly donated to local charities.

In August 2015, NPR reported on several school gardening initiatives across the United States. One of these programs is City Blossoms, a nonprofit centered in Washington, D.C., that brings community gardens to schools, community centers, and other urban areas where kids tend to gather. Of the many students working on the garden, Roshawn Little was spotlighted, both for having three years of experience working in the garden at Eastern Senior High School and because of what working in the garden has taught her. She said that gardening has not only encouraged her to try new vegetables but also to bring vegetables home with her, ultimately encouraging her family to buy more produce. Little discussed her family's tendency to eat what is convenient rather than seeking out what is healthy, saying, "We mainly live around liquor and snack stores. There aren't that many grocery stores. They're way out and you have to drive so far … It seems so pointless, when there are snack stores right there."[25]

Getting kids excited about gardening can help them develop both a closer relationship with their food and a better understanding of nutrition.

Environmental Impacts
of Global Food Production

A report published in 2018 by the Food and Agriculture Organization shed light on what many already knew: The global food system takes a harsh toll on the environment. Three-fourths of the world's fresh water supply goes to global food production. Global food production also contributes one-third of the world's greenhouse gas emissions through both food production itself and the incredible amount of transportation required to move food around the world to consumers. Furthermore, global food production is also the leading cause of biodiversity loss across the entire world, leading to the endangerment and ultimate extinction of many plants and animals.

Research indicates that diets that focus on sustainability are not only good for the environment, they also tend to be healthier. According to Irana Hawkins, contributing faculty member at Walden University and sustainability expert, "Local foods are a necessary and important part of our food system ... They can help regenerate the soil and use seeds that have naturally adapted to the local landscape to grow whole plant foods that aide in promoting biodiversity, mitigating climate change, and improving human health."[1]

The connection between sustainability and health is most apparent when comparing meat and plant-based proteins. By cutting out meat and dairy alone, farmland could be reduced by more than 75 percent and still allow enough food to be grown to feed the world. While meat and dairy provide only 18 percent of the world's calories, they use 83 percent of the world's farmland and produce 60 percent of agriculture's greenhouse gas emissions.

1. Quoted in Chris Vogliano, "In Support of the Local Food Movement," University Health News, March 27, 2018. universityhealthnews.com/topics/nutrition-topics/support-local-food-movement/.

The Little family's experience is not unique. Many families in low-income, urban areas face this same issue. Building nutritional knowledge at a young age is only half the battle; the other half is providing access to affordable food.

The Produce Gap

While farmers' markets are an excellent place to purchase locally grown produce and get to know local farmers, these venues often primarily serve one demographic: white, middle-to-upper class, highly educated consumers. With the emergence of urban food deserts—areas with high levels of racial segregation and income inequality as well as limited access to healthy food sources—changes in the local food movement must be made to ensure that access to healthy food becomes a possibility to all the people who live in an area.

For many low-income people, lack of access to reliable transportation causes traveling short distances to become much more difficult, especially if they have to carry a lot of items. Due to issues such as traveling expenses, traveling with children or a disability, the varying schedules or directness of public transportation, and the weight and logistics of carrying goods back home, traveling a long way for anything other than what is absolutely necessary becomes too difficult to do. Just as with Roshawn Little's family, it becomes easier to visit local snack stores and seems pointless to travel anywhere else for food that will be eaten a few minutes after it arrives home. These circumstances make low-income neighborhoods some of the areas affected most by the diseases caused by a poor diet.

One way to increase the amount of local produce in low-income areas is to bring the farmers' market to the food desert itself. Another way to promote farmers' markets among low-income consumers is to place markets close to transportation hubs. As food trucks have become more common, some farmers' markets are also going mobile. This would allow consumers in many different low-income neighborhoods access to fresh, local fruits and vegetables.

However, while a mobile market seems like a good idea, it is not a magical solution. A study conducted by the Agricultural Marketing Service under the USDA showed that in order for mobile markets to truly make a difference for low-income consumers, there are a few factors that must be taken under consideration. First, there needs to be a solid backing of the program through a partnering organization that provides some type of assistance, whether it is a nonprofit with a lot of volunteers or a hospital or other business that can provide financial support. Another essential element of a successful mobile market is being aware of the

For many low-income families with limited transportation options, convenience stores such as this one are their best shopping option. However, in such stores, it is difficult or impossible to find healthy foods.

community itself—its people and its needs. Employees of a mobile market or its backing organization would need to work to build relationships and trust between the organizations and the people who actually live in the neighborhood. They would also have to make sure the mobile market is able to deliver almost everything the people in a neighborhood need. For example, the REC mobile market in Worcester, Massachusetts, offers not only fresh produce, but also other popular items such as bread, cheese, tea, and honey. This makes people more likely to visit the mobile market because many low-income households do not have the time to buy groceries from more than one store. The more people visit a market, the more likely it is to make enough money to stay open and continue providing service to a community.

Finally, and perhaps most importantly, the mobile market must remain affordable. The U.S. government provides food assistance to low-income families; the two most common programs are the Special Supplemental Nutrition Program for Women, Infants, and Children (WIC) and the Supplemental Nutrition Assistance Program (SNAP). These are sometimes simply called "food stamp" programs because in the past, food assistance came in the form of paper stamps. By 2002, however, these had been replaced in every state by electronic benefit transfer (EBT) cards, which can be swiped at the register like credit cards. The most successful mobile markets accept payment through WIC or SNAP; some even offer matching programs. For example, Civic Works in Baltimore, Maryland, not only accepts WIC and SNAP but also offers a "double dollars" program that matches the amount customers are able to spend with their assistance benefits up to $10.

To make the local food movement accessible to all, it needs to be able to change based on people's needs. Local food advocates should work to promote ongoing

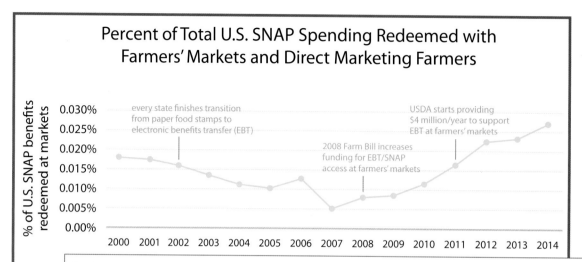

Percent of Total U.S. SNAP Spending Redeemed with Farmers' Markets and Direct Marketing Farmers

% of U.S. SNAP benefits redeemed at markets

0.030%
0.025%
0.020%
0.015%
0.010%
0.005%
0.00%

2000 2001 2002 2003 2004 2005 2006 2007 2008 2009 2010 2011 2012 2013 2014

every state finishes transition from paper food stamps to electronic benefits transfer (EBT)

2008 Farm Bill increases funding for EBT/SNAP access at farmers' markets

USDA starts providing $4 million/year to support EBT at farmers' markets

An increase in the number of farmers' markets accepting EBT payments has made a huge difference in terms of providing low-income families with access to healthy food, as this information from the Farmers Market Coalition shows.

community-based health efforts that emphasize the importance of fresh food but also encourage ongoing practical nutrition education. One way to do this is to offer cooking classes or hand out recipe cards that show people exactly how to substitute healthy foods for unhealthy ones in their cooking.

You Are What You Eat

It is clear that everything people do is affected by what they eat, including how much energy they have and how long that energy lasts, the rate at which they grow and heal themselves, and the ways they stay healthy or the ways they become diseased. It is an important part of the health of a person's blood, bones, and organs. Because food is such an important part of everyday life and general health, we truly are what we eat. In order to avoid becoming tired and sick, we must eat what we know is healthy.

Doctors, nutritionists, and other food experts agree that while everyone's body is different and there is no single best amount of each food to eat, people generally must center their diet around unprocessed, whole foods to create and fuel a healthy body. They emphasize how important it is

Eating Wild

Humans have hunted and gathered since before the development of agriculture, but with the convenience and reliability of farmed food, hunting and gathering is no longer a main source of food. However, just as locally grown foods have become more popular, so has the act of foraging—gathering plants or animals to serve as bait, goods to sell, or food to eat. Chefs around the world who want to combat the industrialized system of the global food market have helped popularize this foraging trend. There are even a growing number of urban foragers who locate food growing in cities. Many of these food items are frequently mistaken for simple weeds.

In Denmark, chef René Redzepi is working to get teenagers involved in foraging. Redzepi's Wild Food project looks to encourage young people to explore the wilderness for ingredients in the hopes that they will find free, healthy foods and recognize the importance of preserving the natural world. Redzepi believes the program has been a success. He gave one example:

> *I took a 7th grade class out to pick garlic mustard, and one of the students told us that he has these plants growing in front of his door and that he'd go talk with his grandma, so that she could go out and use them. He made the connection that his grandma does all the cooking and that these plants are right outside [his house]. That's just great.*[1]

While foraging is an interesting way to connect with the land, identifying fungi and plants can be difficult, so it is important for people to consult an expert before attempting any foraging by themselves.

1. Quoted in Paul Sauer, "René Redzepi Wants to Teach Teenagers How to Forage," *Vice*, June 29, 2017. munchies.vice.com/en_us/article/59zn3q/rene-redzepi-wants-to-teach-teenagers-how-to-forage.

to eat vegetables, fruits, whole grains, and low-fat dairy products; include a moderate amount of lean meats, fish, beans, and eggs; and try to avoid excessive saturated fats, sodium, and added sugars. While eating locally is not the only way to maintain a healthy diet, it is a good way for someone to develop a stronger relationship to the food they eat and the land it comes from.

When asked in a 2017 interview with the *Washington Post* whether Americans' eating habits were moving in the right direction, Michael Jacobson,

The best way to prevent diet-based disease is to eliminate most processed food and learn to cook with whole, healthy ingredients.

cofounder of the Center for Science in the Public Interest and the man who popularized the term "junk food," responded optimistically:

> *Oh, absolutely. Just look at a grocery store. In the 1970s, few even had whole-grain bread or canned chickpeas or yogurt. Now you have to walk through a huge product section to get to that stuff, and there's a large selection … Millions of people just automatically buy whole grains or low-fat dairy products. Meat consumption, specifically beef and pork consumption, has gradually declined over the last 40 years. These things are great for health … Overall, I think we've had a great impact. But there is still more to do, and I look forward to that.*[26]

A Closer Look

According to Teaching Tolerance, a project of the Southern Poverty Law Center, 23.5 million people in the U.S. live in low-income areas more than a mile from a supermarket.

Americans still have a long way to go in terms of solving all the problems of their standard diet, but with increased transparency on the subject of nutrition and the development of affordable and accessible produce for all, there is hope on the horizon.

NOTES

Introduction: Eating Right?

1. Dana E. King, Arch G Mainous III, and Mark E. Geesey, "Turning Back the Clock: Adopting a Healthy Lifestyle in Middle Age," *American Journal of Medicine*, vol. 120, 2007, p. 603. www.amjmed.com/article/S0002-9343(06)01185-5/pdf.

Chapter One: Food as Medicine: Understanding Nutrition

2. "Food Science Terms," Cookery Teacher, accessed on June 4, 2019. thecookeryteacher.com/foodie-terms/frame.php?id=4.

3. Quoted in Carey Goldberg, "Vitamin Reality Check: New Evidence-Based Overview On Who Should Be Taking What," WBUR, February 5, 2018. www.wbur.org/commonhealth/2018/02/05/vitamin-evidence.

4. Aaron Kandola, "Nutrient-Dense Food List," Medical News Today, last updated March 15, 2019. www.medicalnewstoday.com/articles/324713.php.

Chapter Two: Eating Yourself Sick

5. "Interview: Dr. Steven E. Nissen," PBS, August 2006. www.pbs.org/wgbh/takeonestep/heart/interviews-nissen.html.

6. "Interview," PBS.

7. Quoted in Stuart Marsh, "Can You Lose Weight Eating Only Junk Food? Yes, but Here's Why You Shouldn't," 9Coach, December 22, 2015. coach.nine.com.au/2015/12/22/16/47/can-you-lose-weight-eating-only-junk-food.

8. "Diet," National Cancer Institute, April 29, 2015. www.cancer.gov/about-cancer/causes-prevention/risk/diet.

9.   Quoted in "Obesity And Diabetes Double Risk Of Heart Failure: Patients With Both Conditions 'Very Difficult' To Treat," *ScienceDaily*, June 4, 2009. www.sciencedaily.com/releases/2009/05/090530094510.htm.

Chapter Three: A Diet of Healing

10. "The Best Diet: Quality Counts," Harvard T.H. Chan School of Public Health, accessed on June 6, 2019. www.hsph.harvard.edu/nutrition-source/healthy-weight/best-diet-quality-counts/.

11. Quoted in "Longer Life Linked to Specific Foods in Mediterranean Diet," *ScienceDaily*, June 24, 2009. www.sciencedaily.com/releases/2009/06/090624093353.htm.

12. Quoted in "Mediterranean Diet Works by Adding Up Small Improvements," Harvard Health Publishing, March 2019. www.health.harvard.edu/staying-healthy/mediterranean-diet-works-by-adding-up-small-improvements.

13. "Phytochemicals: The Cancer Fighters in Your Foods," American Institute for Cancer Research, accessed on May 10, 2019. www.aicr.org/reduce-your-cancer-risk/diet/elements_phytochemicals.html.

14. Quoted in "Study in 7,000 Men and Women Ties Obesity, Inflammatory Proteins to Heart Failure Risk," Johns Hopkins Medicine, May 1, 2008. www.hopkinsmedicine.org/news/media/releases/study_in_7000_men_and_women_ties_obesity_inflammatory_proteins_to_heart_failure_risk.

15. Quoted in "Phytochemicals in Plant-Based Foods Could Help Battle Obesity, Disease," *ScienceDaily*, October 22, 2009. www.sciencedaily.com/releases/2009/10/091021144251.htm.

16. Quoted in Ann Wang, "Plant Antioxidants also Fight Inflammation," *Johns Hopkins News-Letter*, October 22, 2008. www.jhunewsletter.com/article/2008/10/plant-antioxidants-also-fight-inflammation-30050.

17. Quoted in "Add More Color to Your Diet: At the End of This Rainbow, Plates of Heart-Healthy Foods," HighBeam Research, February 1, 2006. www.highbeam.com/doc/1G1-144106222.html.

18. Quoted in Bev Bennett, "The Green Defense," HighBeam Research, November 8, 2000. www.highbeam.com/doc/1P2-4561974.html.

Chapter Four: Diet Data, Nutritional Advocacy, and Healthy Legislation

19. Quoted in Daniel J. DeNoon, "Metabolic Syndrome Common in Obese Children," WebMD, June 25, 2008. www.webmd.com/children/news/20080625/obese-kids-metabolic-syndrome-common#1.

20. Joseph S. Alpert, "Failing Grades in the Adoption of Healthy Lifestyle Choices," *American Journal of Medicine*, vol. 122, no. 6, June 2009, p. 494. www.amjmed.com/article/S0002-9343(09)00093-X/pdf.

21. Quoted in "Metabolic Syndrome in Children," Aarogya, accessed on June 10, 2019. www.aarogya.com/support-groups/diabetes/metabolic-syndrome-in-children.html.

22. Sheela N. Magge, Elizabeth Goodman, and Sarah C. Armstrong, "The Metabolic Syndrome in Children and Adolescents: Shifting the Focus to Cardiometabolic Risk Factor Clustering," *Pediatrics*, vol. 140, no. 2, August 2017. pediatrics.aappublications.org/content/140/2/e20171603.

23. "Making Fish Protein Available, Accessible, and Affordable in the Philippines," Food and Agricultural Association of the United Nations, accessed on June 10, 2019. www.fao.org/in-action/making-fish-protein-available-accessible-affordable-philippines/it/.

Chapter Five: Food Education

24. Caitlin Dewey, "A Growing Number of Young Americans Are Leaving Desk Jobs to Farm," *Washington Post*, November 23, 2017. www.washingtonpost.com/business/economy/a-growing-number-of-young-americans-are-leaving-desk-jobs-to-farm/2017/11/23/e3c018ae-c64e-11e7-afe9-4f60b5a6c4a0_story.html.

25. Quoted in Paige Pfleger, "Healthy Eaters, Strong Minds: What School Gardens Teach Kids," NPR, August 10, 2015. www.npr.org/sections/thesalt/2015/08/10/426741473/healthy-eaters-strong-minds-what-school-gardens-teach-kids.

26. Quoted in Caitlin Dewey, "How to Fix the American Diet, According to the Man Who Popularized the Term 'Junk Food,'" *Washington Post*, December 28, 2017. www.washingtonpost.com/news/wonk/wp/2017/12/28/how-to-fix-the-american-diet-according-to-the-man-who-coined-the-phrase-junk-food/.

American Cancer Society

250 Williams Street NW

Atlanta, GA 30303

www.cancer.org

www.instagram.com/americancancersociety

twitter.com/americancancer

> The American Cancer Society provides the public with information about every major type of cancer, including causes, symptoms, diagnosis, and treatment. A live chat and Cancer Helpline phone number are available on the website.

American Diabetes Association

2451 Crystal Drive, Suite 900

Arlington, VA 22202

www.diabetes.org

www.instagram.com/AmDiabetesAssn

twitter.com/AmDiabetesAssn

www.youtube.com/user/AmericanDiabetesAssn

> The American Diabetes Association provides information to patients, caregivers, families, health care professionals, and researchers. Its website includes a live chat and a toll-free hotline number for those who have questions about diabetes.

American Public Health Association (APHA)

800 I Street NW

Washington, D.C. 20001

www.apha.org

twitter.com/PublicHealth

> APHA is an organization that works to protect the health of Americans through programs that provide education and preventive health services to communities.

School Nutrition Association

2900 S Quincy Street, Suite 700

Arlington, VA 22206

www.schoolnutrition.org

www.instagram.com/schoolnutritionassoc

twitter.com/SchoolLunch

www.youtube.com/user/SchoolNutrition

> The School Nutrition Association website contains news related to nutrition in schools, such as school lunch and breakfast programs, programs to combat childhood obesity, and legislation related to school nutrition.

United States Department of Agriculture (USDA)

1400 Independence Avenue SW

Washington, D.C. 20250

www.usda.gov

www.instagram.com/usdagov

twitter.com/usda

www.youtube.com/usda

> The USDA provides information about not only agriculture but also nutrition and disease across the United States. Learn more about nutrition laws and regulations and find many other nutritional resources on its website and social media pages.

FOR MORE INFORMATION

Books

Allman, Toney. *Nutrition and Disease Prevention*. New York, NY: Chelsea House, 2010.

   The author explores how the way people eat can contribute to either the development or prevention of disease.

Duyff, Roberta Larson. *American Dietetic Association Complete Food and Nutrition Guide, 4th Edition*. New York, NY: Wiley, 2012.

   This revised version includes updated scientific advice about what foods are best for the body, guidelines for weight control, guidelines for eating healthfully in restaurants, and an explanation of how diet is connected to chronic diseases.

Hughes, Meredith Sayles. *Plants vs. Meats: The Health, History, and Ethics of What We Eat*. Minneapolis, MN: Twenty-First Century Books, 2016.

   Many people choose their food based not only on health but on their beliefs as well. This book explores facts and myths about the health value of certain foods as well as the ethics involved in special diets such as vegetarianism.

Pelkki, Jane Sieving. *Healthy Eating*. New York, NY: Children's Press, 2017.

   This book gives tips about how to eat a healthy diet.

Websites

American Heart Association

www.americanheart.org

> This website includes information about diseases and conditions that are caused by cardiovascular disease as well as news about research being done in this area, advice concerning a healthy diet and lifestyle, and a section devoted to children's health.

Nutrition.gov

www.nutrition.gov

> The federal government's website on nutrition includes information provided by the USDA, the Department of Health and Human Services, and other government agencies. It contains links to information about weight management, the dietary guidelines for Americans, and the safety of vitamin and mineral supplements.

Self Nutrition Data

nutritiondata.self.com

> This website, run by *Self* magazine, offers tools such as a food tracker, BMI calculator, and database of foods sorted by nutrient—for instance, someone can search for foods that are high in vitamin C and low in sugar.

USDA: National Farmers' Market Directory

www.ams.usda.gov/local-food-directories/farmersmarkets

> This directory provides convenient and comprehensive information about local food vendors in a particular area.

INDEX

PICTURE CREDITS

ABOUT THE AUTHOR

Holly Brown is a writer, teacher, farmer, and librarian who lives in Cleveland, Ohio. She loves cooking and eating, traveling to new places, and making friends with every cat she meets.